Callum's Shenanigans and Mishaps

(Memories from the Croft and Beyond)

By Malcolm Macleod

Copyright © 2022 Malcolm Macleod

All rights reserved.

ISBN: 9798443061085

DEDICATION

I wish to dedicate this book to Valerie, my wife for over fifty years who has bravely battled Cancer for the past twenty years, my son Robert and my daughter Karen, who have both left the nest and made their own way in life, with little help from me.

Also, my friends Patrick and Peggy Broe, who helped me tremendously with hints and ideas for the layout and the publication of this book.

Heartfelt thanks.

Introduction

Life goes by in the blink of an eye and the world it keeps on changing.

The times we've lived through and the people we knew, fade away like the sun sinks below the horizon.

Through these simple tales and anecdotes, I hope to bring times gone by, back into focus. Breathe life back into the characters, coves and blones, who shared in my adventures.

Let's remember our own stories, our disasters and glories, the times and the people who made us.

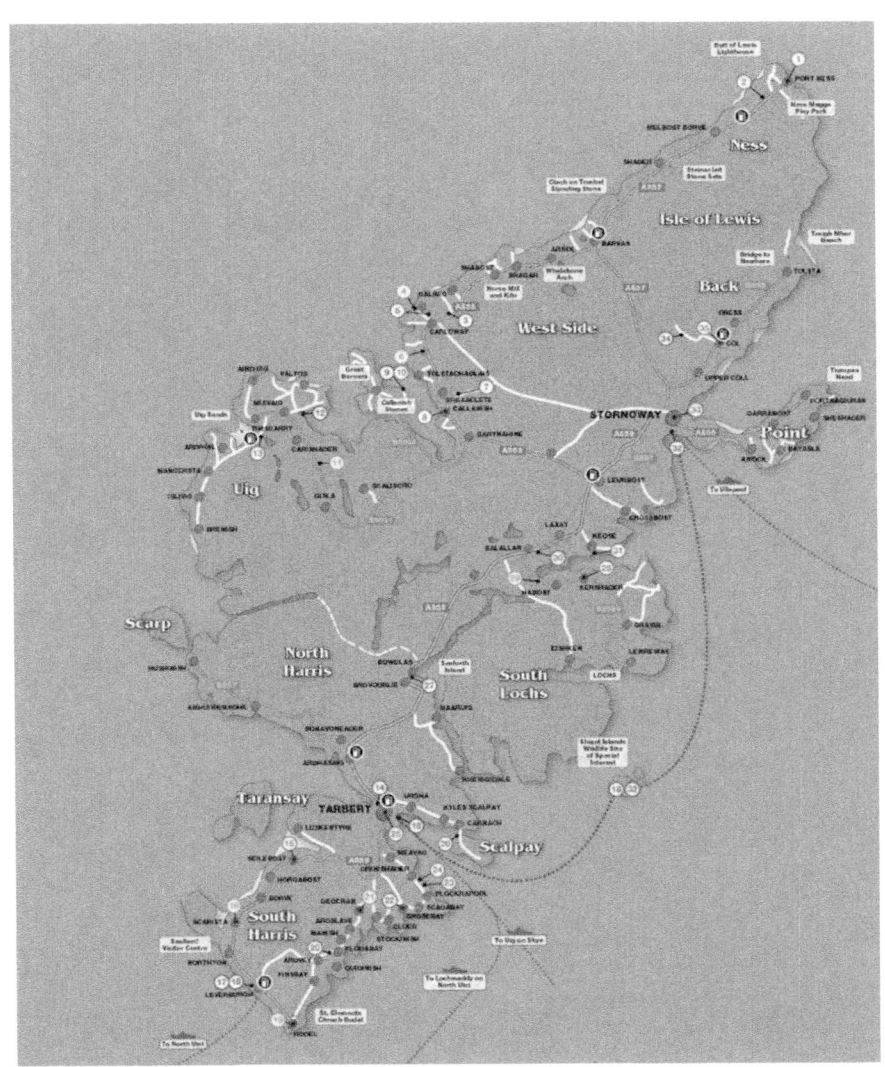

CONTENTS

	Memory	12
1	Early Memories	15
2	Growing Up	29
3	My Teens	38
4	London Bound	49
5	Marriage and Beyond	68
6	Northern Ireland	75
7	Homeward Bound	92
8	Moving On	102
9	Hospital Appointments	110
10	Redundancy to Self-Employment	117
11	Tales from my Elders	120
12	My Mad Days	123
	Closing Thoughts	127
	Family Tree	129

Memory

For as long as I live

All the people I've loved

Are right here

accessible to me

They remain bright and clear

They can always be near

Through the wonderful lens

Of memory

As our time matches On

The path we've walked along

Is littered with streetlights

Of memories

We know we've been here

And who we've been near

Thanks to our personal

Biographer

Memory

The joy and the pain

They have both

Been our gain

From pages and chapters

Written with others

They've developed the plot

Fleshed out characters

Helped when we were lost

Those beautiful

Sisters and brothers

As we think back

On them

Let's remember again

That we appear

In other peoples

Stories

So, let's pick up

The pen

Write the next line with them

Leave them access to

Wonderful memories

Used with kind permission Patrick Broe from his book, Perspectives

1 Early Memories

Growing up on the shores of Loch Erisort with the estuary of the best salmon river in the Isle-of-Lewis at the bottom of our croft giving me plenty of opportunity to explore the world into which I was born. My earliest memory is playing with my next-door neighbour Callum, when I was about four years old. He was a month younger than me. I don't recall what we were playing, but I was running after him, and the next thing my legs got tangled in a ram's horn which was lying on the ground, down I went. My head hit a stone and split open just above my left eye, you can still see the scar today. my mother took me to the local doctor, two stitches later!

Going into school was something I did not fancy, you had to take a peat with you for the fire to keep the place warm. This changed shortly afterwards, as the parents volunteered to cut a stack that would last all year. During the first week I decided for some unknown reason it was not for me, and decided to run home alone, all two miles of it- there were no buses then and very few cars. Eventually I noticed that nobody else seemed to go home at that time, so I decided to stay and see what would happen. I came to like it and we had some fun, especially after school in the hot weather when the tar was melting on the road. We would leave our bare footprints in the tar and walk home with our sandshoes tied round our necks. On arriving home my mother would chastise me and try to get the tar off my feet with margarine, at that time the only thing available that would melt tar. I did not like the thought of getting that done and one day managed to avoid her and went to bed. I was quite happy until next morning when I couldn't get out of bed as the bed sheets were stuck to my body and naturally my mother was not very happy, nor my father, as they had to buy new sheets.

One morning a pupil who was a few years older than me went into the cloakroom and found his classmate hanging by his collar on a coat hook with his legs swinging in the air and going blue in the face. He somehow managed to get him down and revive him. Two older pupils had hung him up for a prank.

I have a vague memory of my mother cooking on an open fire as we did not have a stove as that was before the kitchen was built. In the spring, my mother would get the blankets and take them in a creel to the river, which was approximately half a mile away. I had to go with her as she had a job for me. As some blankets were made of Harris Tweed and very heavy. There was a big cast iron pot left out for anybody in the village to use, I don't recall what it was called but I know there was a name for it. My first job was to collect some dry peat and start a fire under the pot, and then get some water from the river to fill it. Once it was about half full and the water getting warm, the blankets were put in the pot to be washed. The next thing I knew I was lifted into the pot as well. There were two reasons for this, first I was to trample the blankets to get them washed the other was I was getting my feet washed or was I!! I was lifted out smelling of smoke, thankfully before the water got too hot. This process took two or three days, once they were washed, they were lifted out and spread on the heather to dry and would be collected the next day or the following day.

The winters were something else, we lived in a two up two down house and when the gales came, we huddled in bed with every sheet and blanket we could find wrapped around us. The skylight was tied down in case it blew off along with the slates, some days I thought the bed was shaking as well. We were taught how to do things from an early age, and I remember my mother weeding and thinning the turnips. I was walking behind her picking up the seeds she had dropped not realising that they were left behind for a reason. Once she realized what I was doing, I got a wee smack on the wrist and told to go and play somewhere else. Attending primary school taught me that if you misbehaved there were consequences, you were given the tawse (the strap), quite often it was somebody else doing the misbehaving and every now and then the tawse would disappear. Whilst the teacher was out of the room, there would be a mad scramble to get to the teacher's desk to get the tawse before she came back. We would throw it up to a narrow window near the ceiling. It was a long-lost battle because as soon as she found out it was missing there would be a new one the following morning. When it came to putting up the Christmas decorations there would be plenty of volunteers to go up the ladder to that window, somebody would distract the teacher and the tawse would be down somebody's trousers then thrown into a loch on the way home. Getting the strap in school did not do us any harm in fact it probably helped us take the right direction in life.

We had some severe winters and 1954-55 we had very heavy snow up to 5- or 6-foot drifts. We were off school for about six weeks; I was ten and remember opening the back door and all I could see was a wall of snow. I fetched the fire side shovel and where originally there was one step down to the pavement, I had to form three steps up to get out of the house. My father was out all day trying to save his sheep, he was able to locate them, as there was a hole in the snow where they were breathing. The postman, when he eventually came was quite tall and wore big wellington boots, where he left prints in the snow, we would jump from one to the other peeking over the top to spot where we had been. This reminds me of an old pigmy tribe found in the Australian bush called the flick are we tribe, as they used to jump up and down shouting where the flick are we. I saw a photo of Goathill Road in Stornoway, it showed the area blanketed in snow with just the tops of the trees, the ridges and chimneys of the houses showing. It took them two weeks to clear using two tractors. I was walking to school on a windy day, about twenty yards behind my sister when I spotted a sheet of zinc flying towards her. if I hadn't noticed this and shouted to her, I am sure she would have been beheaded. There were plenty of snowmen made as well with a competition for the biggest. Sledging in the snow was fun, we used to pull our sledges up the hill and then take off, and the snow would sometimes be up to the top of the fence. The drifts were so high, with just the top wire showing. We would shoot over them, how we survived passing over that wire without injury I don't know because if we had gone under the wire we would have been cut in half. We didn't have a care in the world-all good fun!

Before the water was piped to the house, I had to bring the water from the well. My mother would send me to the well with two buckets and by the time I arrived back I had only two half buckets, so she would send me back again, we could empty the well of water and within twenty minutes it was full of crisp clear water, much better than the water you get now from a tap. My mother would send me to the shop for some groceries," get me half dozen eggs, quarter pounds of tea, a loaf of bread and two pounds of sugar, will you remember that"? "Yes", I said, and took off. The shop was only half a mile away, and as I walked, I kept repeating over and over in my head the list of what I had to ask for. Well by the time I arrived, after being distracted by various things my shopping list went something like this. Two pounds of bread, half a dozen pounds of tea and a pound of eggs. My aunt, who owned the shop, was in stitches but eventually worked out what my mother wanted.

Another game we played going to school was kick the welly, it involved removing your foot halfway out and kicking your leg in the air to see who would go farthest. My brother was quite good at this until one day going to school he tried it and landed in the loch beside the road and had to go to school wearing one wellington- you can just imagine the schoolmaster's thoughts, This didn't put him off, as that weekend he tried it at the back of the house and went straight through the only pane of glass in the byre, guess who got the blame as he was nowhere to be found?

My father had a double barrel shotgun, and I remember him running in for it when he saw a flock of geese going by, he took aim and let both barrels go and three of them fell to the ground, we ate well that week. We also did a lot of fishing, I used to go with my father and an old neighbour to lay the nets. We would come home with sacks full of Haddock, Cod, Ling, Flounders. A variety of fish, we would place them in piles at the end of the house, I had to turn my back and my father would point to a pile, ask who it was going to, I had to answer without looking. I had to go around the village delivering fish. Sometimes we would get so many, my father would salt them and put them in barrels. Quite often my mother would make (Cearn Cropaig) which is fish liver and oatmeal stuffed in a fish head and baked. I tried making it a few years back it was very nice but not (like mama used to make) and I have mislaid the recipe.   Fly fishing was great fun trailing the line behind the boat and catching Mackerel, if you had two or three on the line, they would nearly pull you out of the boat they were so strong.

One day my father decided he would visit a friend in Habost about half an hour's row across loch Erisort, so I went with him. It was about ten o'clock at night when my father decided it was time to leave and as we left the house heading back to the boat you couldn't see your hand in front of your face. The fog had come down. My father's friend suggested that we should stay, and he would get us home by road. Dad wouldn't hear of it; all we needed was a torch, I had to sit in the bow to light our way and off we went. I thought afterwards if we did hit anything I would be the first to go. After rowing for a while my father told me to put my hand in the water and Low and behold within a few minutes I felt this thing in the water and made a grab for it, our mooring rope. To this day I do not know how he found his way, as we couldn't see the stars because of the fog. He had an outboard engine for the boat, which was great. One day as he was cleaning it, he asked me to hold two wires for him, one in each hand to see if there was a spark in it. When he pulled on the starting cord the charge went through my body and as I nearly hit the ceiling I screamed, let go of the wires and shot out the door like a dog after a rabbit. I never pestered my father again and stayed well clear of engines.

We used to snare rabbits as they made quite a tasty dinner. However once myxomatosis appeared on the island, that put a stop to that. After school I used to stop off to see my grandmother, Hannah, my mother's mother. I'd help my uncle Archie bring in the peats and help with the hay. Sometimes I would have to stay with her when my uncle went to church as in later years, she was bedridden. She died when I was about seventeen. She was the first person I ever saw in a coffin. I was seven or eight when my father's father died, I can only remember him being in bed in his last years. He had been a leading seaman during the First World War. His name was Malcolm, he enrolled in April 1899. He reported to HMS Pembroke on 3rd August 1914, following six weeks of training he was posted to the armed, merchant cruiser HMS Orama, which patrolled the Pacific. Here is an extract from the ships log, dated 11th November 1914:

Ship's Log for HMS Orama

Montevideo to Abrolhos Rocks

Lat -34.6, Long -53.5

5.10am: Lobos Island Lighthouse abeam

3.47pm: Observed steamer heading ESE; altered course to examine same

4.10pm: Full speed; strange ship apparently being set on fire

5.15pm: Stop alongside German Fleet Auxiliary Navarra badly on fire and crew in ship's boats

5.25pm: Took crew on board

6.15pm: Proceeded, manoeuvring ship for firing at GFA Navarra

7.38pm: GFA Navarra turned turtle and sank in 35 fathoms water – Lat 34 40S Long 52 43W

11.30pm: Prisoners inspected hourly

The Orama was sunk by U62, a German submarine, on 19th October 1917, with no loss of life. This shows the hardship and brutality that they endured during World War one, while patrolling the North and South Pacific. Something we can't comprehend in our time, and this was just one day in his life.

He joined HMS Vindictive in 1916 but after six weeks he went on sick leave with a varicose vein problem. He later served on the armed merchant cruiser HMS Edinburgh Castle. He had been on board the HMS Edinburgh Castle patrolling the North and South Pacific, but He escaped being on board when she was sunk, just South of Ireland, as he was dropped off in England prior to it being torpedoed. He had a miraculous escape on his home voyage after the war. He was one of 283 islanders on board the steam yacht, Iolaire, Gaelic word for Eagle, within sight of home on New Year's Eve 1918, when the ship hit the rocks, known locally as the Beasts of Holm. 205 men died that night, only 73 survived, most of them, including grandad, pulled themselves ashore on a rope secured by John F Macleod, an islander from Ness. This was a national tragedy but a devastating blow to the island community. My mother told me that when he reached dry land, he only had the little finger of his right hand on the rope. Since then, that finger was always half closed couldn't be straightened. My mother who was about fourteen at the time was in town a couple of days later and asked if certain people were on the boat and had they survived. She was told that some of her cousins had not survived. Imagine surviving four years of war then losing your life twenty yards from your own home. A very sad day for the whole island.

When I was eight or ten years old the villagers bought a boat that was due to be scrapped. I remember standing on a chair to look out of the skylight, seeing my father towing this massive hulk with his boat using the outboard engine. sailing into the loch to the river estuary, where it was beached. The villagers stripped all the timber to use as posts and strainers for their croft- I think the only thing remaining is the engine which you can still see to this day. She was called The Speedwell.

On Guy Fawkes night we had some fun, we would collect old tires, dead trees and anything that would burn then take them up to the top of Navir, the highest hill in the neighbourhood. We persuaded one fellow who had a tractor to take a tree that had fallen up to the fire. This kept us occupied for weeks before hand. Once the fire was started you looked out for other fires, some as far away as Harris, Point, and Barvas. I don't know if young people nowadays know who Guy Fawkes was or the story behind it.

My father had a horse when I was very young. I don't remember its name, but I remember being on its back with my legs out like a ballerina. Most of the land was used either for hay, potatoes, corn, or vegetables. This was another chore we had to do. my father used to sit me on the (cliath) to put some weight on when he was planting the corn. A (cliath)is a four foot by four-foot steel frame with three- or four-inch spikes protruding from underneath, which the horse pulled behind him. He also had a two wheeled tractor that you walked behind- it wouldn't go any faster than five miles an hour. Eventually he had a trailer made for it and we could sit on it and bring in the hay. Planting and lifting the potatoes, planting turnips, and then having to thin them as they grew, hoeing the potatoes, all chores I had to do in my teenage years. We also had to build peat stacks when the peat was brought in from the moor. One year my father had three or four haystacks, and I think four corn stacks, that was a lot of work that year. When the corn was ripe, my father would cut it down with the scythe and we had the job of lifting it, then making them into sheaves and standing them to dry then placing them into stacks. Once we took the stacks down to store in the byre, we had the dogs and cats on standby, as when we came to the bottom it was full of rat holes, so we got buckets of hot water and poured them down the holes and watch them as they came up, and the dog and cats were chasing them, that was good fun. The problem with the hay was having the weather to dry it, one year it wouldn't stop raining but my father was determined. He brought all the hay to the end of the house and spread it on the ground and kept an eye on the weather. He knew that dry weather was coming with some wind, ideal for drying hay. Then sure enough at two o clock in the morning, the rain stopped, and a slight wind came up. Dad got up, plugged in an extension cable put the bedside lamp out through the window and started on the hay. When we got up in the morning, he had it all dry. People from across the loch phoned my aunt next morning asking if everything was alright at our house, as they could see an unusual light at the end of the house and some activity. Along with the horse there were two or three cows to tend to and the sheep. Another chore was to get the cows out to the moor and collect them in the evening, I was also taught how to milk the cow, which came in handy if I felt thirsty and fancied a cup of milk and there was none in the house. Instead of waiting for my mother to milk the cow, I would run over to the byre with a cup and get enough for a drink, which was nice and warm. Whenever a cow calved the first milking was kept for making cheese, and any sour cream was made into butter nothing was wasted. Sometimes when I got home from school, my mother would have a job for me, making the butter. There were two types of churns, one on which you turned a handle, on the other you used a plunger. I had to sit at the table and turn the handle until the butter started forming. I have a vague memory that when too much was made, it was wrapped tightly in cloth put in a casket and sealed, then my father would bury it in the ground to preserve it. It would stay fresh for weeks, to mark where it was buried, he would place a certain stone on top. Afterwards I thought, why not put a cross beside it with the words (here lies mothers butter). As there were no fridges then the milk was kept in a bottle submerged in a bucket of water and left in the coolest area of the house. Whenever a sheep was killed nothing was wasted, from the head which had a lot of meat on it, to the trotters, the intestines were cleaned and made into black and white pudding with the blood, and other ingredients. Every few days, I would be told to collect the eggs from the hen shed, if there were none, it meant they had laid there eggs somewhere else in the garden, and I had to find them. If we had a broody hen, my mother showed me how to pick the eggs to put under the hen, by holding the egg up to the light, in those days you used a torch, then you can see which were fertile, and which were not.

My father was also a weaver as most of the island folk were at that time, but in his younger days he went to Patagonia in South America to work on the sheep farms as a lot of island folk did, as there was little work on the island. Some nights when somebody came in for a visit I would sit in and listen to their stories, some of which I recall and mention here. Each man had to take a dog with him as they had to work on a farm, one man did not have a dog and when he was told this he panicked, so as soon as they berthed in Ullapool to pick up more passengers, he saw somebody with a terrier and bought it. I always wondered how that terrier got on with the sheep. Sometimes they took two- or three-days riding on horseback from the farm to a hut to look after the sheep, the place was so vast. On wild wintry nights that kept me indoors I would be looking at old photos some with my father on horseback and with the sheep. One photo I remember, it was postcard size and showed a man on horseback in the middle and the rest were sheep, you could not see the ground or the sky, there were thousands of sheep. Unfortunately, a lot of these photos were lent to others and were supposed to be returned, but sadly were not. Although I have come across some of them in various books. Growing up I had a rug beside my bed and I realised it was different from other rugs, it was rectangular or circular but I could see that it was a reptile skin, I asked my mother what it was, she said it was something my father brought back from South America, but could not tell me what it was called .As soon as he came in, I asked him, and he told me it was the skin of an Iguana from South America which is like a large lizard, I don't know if he had shot and skinned it himself or not, it was about three feet by two feet in size, it was probably shot for food as the meat is white like chicken, and it was a week's ride on horseback to the nearest ranch for food (going down the road to the supermarket was not an option) or it may have been attacking or scaring the lambs. I wish I had listened to their stories, instead of going out with my mates. I can imagine my father's reaction coming across that for the first time, the only wild animal he saw on the croft was a rat or a rabbit. I remember him mentioning Tierra del Fuego which is probably the port where he boarded the ship to come home.

While learning to ride a bike, we had some hilarious moments. The only bike around belonged to a neighbour, an old BSA and the saddle was level with my shoulder, so the only way to peddle was with my right leg under the crossbar. Hector and I used to take turns riding in and out of the road. Eventually we were able to sit on the saddle if the other person held the bike. There was one problem, when you cycled out the road there was no one there to help you, when you wanted to come off and turn around. We soon found a solution to that problem, there was a clump of raised earth on one side of the road, high enough to put our foot on it and not fall over, that worked well for a while until one day Hector went too fast and missed his footing. Next thing he was over the handlebars and into the drain at the side of the road. The drain was at least five feet deep and full of stagnant water, black sludge that stank of goodness knows what, lucky for him I saw it happening and ran like mad to help. When I saw the bike, there was only half of the rear wheel showing, it had toppled on top of him, into the drain. I pulled desperately on the bike to find him, goodness knows where I got the strength, and eventually it came up, with Hector hanging on to the front wheel. I can laugh at it now, but at the time, I had to lay him on the road and try to clean his mouth so he could breath and clean his eyes as he couldn't see a thing, Finally he got to his feet and we made our way up to his granny's where he was staying, She must have seen us coming because she met us at the door , the first thing she said was strip, no way are you coming in the house like that. Hector had to strip down to his birthday suit, and I believe they had to hose him down as well as his clothes, before he jumped into the bath, that put a stop to that malarkey for a while.

We soon got the hang of things with the bike and went everywhere on it. My older brother bought a bike from the co-op, and I soon took charge of it. Once someone left a bike at keose road end, and would we go to collect it, I volunteered to take the bike in my right hand and off we went, bad idea, I was half way down the hill going like the clappers, when I realised the brakes I needed were on my right the one holding the other bike, there was nothing for it I had to pull my front brakes, you can imagine what happened next, the two front wheels came together and I went over the handlebars, and nearly landed in a loch. This was not the first, or last time I went over the handlebars. Hector and I went up to Balallan one night, we only had one bike I was peddling and had him on the crossbar. It was pitch dark, although we had a torch on the bike it was of no use. there were no streetlights then. Coming down the hill at the school I felt this thing brushing my hand, and then all I could hear was some cursing and shouting after us. I don't know if we knocked over the old man or not, but we did not stay around to find out. He couldn't have been badly hurt if he could shout after us like that. Another hilarious moment was when one night as it was just getting dark and a crowd of us were cycling through the village but this night, we took a trip off the main road and went through the village. As we went by a house and down the road, Callum, my next door neighbour, was about ten yards in front of me, suddenly his bike stopped and he went flying over the handlebars and he landed on his back in the drain, all he could say was,(the bike stopped) we could not stop laughing, Somebody had put up a fence to keep the sheep from wandering off and as it was getting dark we hadn't seen it. I was out one night on the main road with my bike playing around with a few others, when a big black van stopped beside us. Wondering who it was I looked up, and saw **Police** written on the side of it. knowing that we didn't have any lights on the bikes we took off, on the peat road as fast as we could, with a policeman chasing us, until he got fed up and shouted for us to get lights on our bikes. Another time I went out to see my mates, and found them up at the cemetery, there is a steep hill leading up to it. One of us had bought a second-hand racing bike, the one with low handlebars, and I asked for a shot of it, and I left him my own. I jumped on and peddled furiously down the hill, only to hear shouting from behind, **"there are no brakes on it",** you can imagine what happened next. I was heading for the main road, and if any cars came, I was a goner. I was going too fast to turn onto the road so nothing for it, over the road into the fence, over the handlebars over the fence I went and landed on my back in the heather on the other side. From then on, I made sure that my bike had brakes. Every so often, when I left the house, I used to peddle down to the gate, pull the brakes on, so that I would slide sideways, pull the bolt of the gate, and open it without coming of the bike. As I went through the gate would swing closed on its own. Well that was what was supposed to happen, but not this time, as I came up to the gate, and pulled on both brakes both brakes snapped, I went over the handlebars, and the funny thing which I can't explain, I landed on my feet with my hands over my shoulders hanging onto the gate, if I had landed any other way I would have been in a terrible mess. Looking back at the bike I thought it had its day, the front wheel and the actual frame was like the letter z. As I am writing these stories, other things come to mind. As a teenager catching seagulls, we would prop up a basin or bucket with a stick, leave some fish under it then tie a string to the stick and go and hide. When the seagull came for the fish, we pulled the stick away to trap it. The problem then was getting a hold of the seagull without getting bitten, and when they bite you, they always drew blood. Fishing off the rocks for Cuddies was great, and going up the river with a gaff, to see if we saw some salmon. A gaff is a length of stick with a large hook tied at one end. When you saw a salmon you stuck the hook in and pulled it ashore. Playing football as a teenager, we used our jackets as goal posts. The football we had was not as light as the ones we have today, it was made of real leather, and as it got wet it became heavier, by the end of the day you could not kick it you dragged it into goal. Sometimes when you kicked it, the ball would be so heavy it stayed where it was, and you went flying over it. That was the time to go home, you took the ball with you and put it beside the fire to dry out, ready for tomorrow. I played a few games for the school team trying for the Kemney cup, and for the team at work, I don't remember winning any games for them, I don't think they ever won a game. Beside us was a black house, which was occupied by a brother and sister. The living area was at one end of the building and the animals were kept at the other end. Whenever I visited, I would enter through the door at the animal's end. I'm not sure if the cows were pleased to see me as every time, I pushed passed them, they would swish their tails so that I had to dodge them. I had to avoid their deposits on the floor to. Once past this hurdle I would open the door into the living area and shout to see where they were. It was very hard to see in there, as the place was filled with smoke from the fire in the middle of the room. It wasn't a palace, nor even a healthy place to live but they were happy there, it was all they had ever known.

2 Growing Up

When I was about fourteen, I joined the army cadets, that was fun, we had drill in the local hall every Thursday night and occasionally over in town. We were taught how to march, salute and how to hold a rifle plus how to move along the ground without being seen. It wasn't heather we crawled through but the biggest bunch of nettles you ever saw. I had nettle rash for days after that! We were told that if you ever dropped your rifle, you might as well drop with it. Well, it would only happen to me as we stood at attention, I felt my rifle slipping from my grasp and heard the clatter on the floor. I closed my eyes, and fell on top of it, pretending that I had fainted. Panic ensued, they tried to open my collar, wet my face with a sponge, then sat me in a chair. If I'd admitted what had happened my life wouldn't be worth living, it was years later that I owned up to the truth. We were camping on the mainland one year; I think it was down in Newark in the borders. The ferry left at four in the morning, so we hadn't slept much that night, trying to find a seat became impossible. I climbed up to the top deck, and found some slatted seats, stretched out there with my big army coat over me and slept like a log. It rained hard throughout the night, but my coat kept me dry, I think it took six months for it to dry out. I woke up as we were about to berth and found the rest of the crowd running around, they thought I had fallen overboard as there had been a roll call and I was missing. On arrival at camp, we were put in Nissan huts, and given camp beds to sleep in. we were permitted leave, to take a look at the local town but had to walk five miles to get there, at least we could get a bus back. The whole battalion marched off to town. Four of us found ourselves in an open-air market, it was huge, and we couldn't find our way out. We had entered along a narrow alleyway and there were a few of them, finding the right one was the problem. Eventually, we found our way out and caught the bus just as it was leaving. Some of the others were not so lucky, they were delivered to the camp by local police throughout the day and they were given extra duties the following day. One day a storm blew up, it was pouring with rain and drill was postponed. The road was flooded with about four inches of rainwater it was like a river. We managed to cross over to another hut to play cards or darts; after a while two cadets started a pillow fight, as they stood on their beds fighting, there was a flash of lightening. The pillows disappeared, and the feathers flew everywhere, the boys were unharmed but very lucky. In all the noise and commotion, the sergeant major looked in and seeing the mess, he was not impressed, we had to pick up all the feathers, which wasn't easy, when you bent down to pick one up, someone would come along and blow it away.

I mentioned earlier the hot summers, I remember Donnie and I walking along the road in our shorts and sandshoes, wishing we could swim to cool down. It must have been in the nineties, I don't recall whose idea it was, but we decided to climb up a hill, there was a loch behind it to see if we could swim, mad or not. Donnie waded out to above his knees, I was I bit braver, up to my chest. After a while I said I would have a go, luckily, I was facing the shore, when I came up for air and found my feet, Donnie was nearly at the top of the hill, shouting for help. He eventually spotted that I had come up and was near the shore but spluttering my guts up, he came back down. I don't know how long I was under water but that was the last time that was attempted.

Salmon poaching was quite common, but only what they call one for the pot. While walking home from a dance one night we heard something splashing in a stream not far off the road. Wearing our best clothes or not we were going to get them, there were two salmon we only got one, but we went home happy.

There was always something to occupy my attention. One of the men in the village had a digger and he had the task of making the river deeper for the fish to get up. Curiosity got the better of me and I went to see what he was doing. As I arrived at the riverbank, he swung the bucket over towards me and told me to jump in so I could get in the cab with him. After a while in the cab watching him working the bucket, he lifted me back to the bank and that was me off home.

I remember being in hospital, aged about eleven, I had been suffering earache for a very long time, and I was going deaf. It was decided to take my tonsils and adenoids out, so I was whipped in for surgery. I was standing in the doorway about ten days later, when suddenly, my ears popped, I had never heard birds singing like that, I could not get over it. One day my father asked my brother to go and bail out the boat as she was well down in the water, when he pulled the boat in, he took off his wellington boots, and rolled his trousers up. As he stepped, in his foot slipped, and he nearly fell overboard, while he steadied himself, he realized it was a salmon he had stood on, the boat was so low in the water when the salmon jumped it landed in the boat, he managed to catch it and throw it ashore. You should have seen the grin on his face, as he walked home with the salmon, and explained how he got it.

Out in the river, in front of our croft, there is an island, known locally as Sgeir an Acair, or anchor island in English. The island is topped by two rocks, with a channel between them in a V shape, at high tide these are submerged. Sometimes this would catch people unawares, particularly villagers from Kershader and Habost, who used to row across on Sundays to church as their boat would become trapped in the channel. As the tide receded, I can remember my father going out in his boat to rescue them.

My cousin and I used to go poaching together, we were living beside the best salmon rivers in the isle-of-Lewis, and it was a natural reaction to try and get one or two for the pot. He had an A35 van and used to keep the net in the back. One night we were driving up and down the road when we met the gamekeeper, he stopped beside us and asked what we were up to, quick as a flash he said , we were waiting for you to go down to the lodge as we had the net in the back ready to go to the river, whether he believed us or not I don't know, he just laughed and drove off, I can't remember how many we got. One night we decided to go out after midnight, we took two sacks, one for the net and one for the fish, if we caught any. My cousin took the net and waded across the river, I stayed on the bank to warn him if the watchers came, we felt a few going into the net, but the next thing we saw was the watchers with their torches. I gave him a signal to warn him, and he waded back over. we tried to get the salmon out of the net but decided it would take too long, as the gamekeepers' men were getting too close. Half the net went into one sack and the other half in the other. Well, the run home from the river was a real comedy act, as we ran, we would come up against a peat bank then had to climb at least three feet then pull the other fellow after you, it was quite hilarious. Once we climbed over one bank, we would run headfirst into another peat bank, all of this with the gamekeepers after us. All we could see were the torches, it was so dark they could hear us but not see us. Once when returning from fishing with my father using the outboard engine on the boat, as we turned towards the croft, one of the clamps holding the engine in place, snapped. The engine slid sideways so that the controls were under water, dad couldn't stop it. We were going through a channel between rocks, and as the engine was on its side and half under water it was acting like a rudder, and we started going round in circles, that is one thing you don't want to do, when you are in the vicinity of rocks, as I warned my father we were heading for the rocks, he managed to swing the engine round the other way, then we would be circling in the opposite direction, every time that happened, we were both flung to the other side of the boat and nearly overboard, after doing a few figure of eights among the rocks, he managed to cut the engine and bring it aboard. I think what saved us was the high tide, although we could still see some rocks above water. If it had been low tide there would be more rocks to avoid, although we were not far from shore, it was too far for me to swim, I don't know if my father could either. at least we survived to live another day. As a teenager catching seagulls. we used to prop up a basin, or bucket, with a stick, leave some fish under it, tie a string to the stick and go and hide, when the seagull came for the fish, we pulled the stick away to trap it, the problem then was getting hold of the seagull without getting bitten, and when they bit you, they always drew blood.

Fishing off the rocks for Cuddies was great, and going up the river with a gaff, to see if we could catch salmon. A gaff is a length of stick with a large hook tied at one end, if you saw salmon, you pushed the hook in and pulled it ashore. We could see the shoal of salmon coming in the loch, when they were trying to go upriver there was a ripple like a V gliding through the water. One year the salmon were afflicted by disease, they became blind, and their heads were white. They were easily caught in the sea as they were trying to find the river, we were told they were fine to eat but not the heads. I don't know if there were many eaten that year.

Planting and lifting the potatoes, harvesting, and drying the hay, cutting, and lifting the peats, all hard back breaking work. These were good times, though tough, the best part was when you had the picnic and your cup of tea on the moor. When it came to peat cutting, four or six men would gather at the house early in the morning, have a cup of tea before leaving for the peat bank, but by the time they had each told their stories it would be late morning. After you had walked out to the peat bank, you would be ready for another cup of tea! Following several weeks of drying out we had to turn them to dry the other side. Finally, when they were ready, we would use tractors to bring them home for stacking. I can still see my mother coming home with a creel full of Peats on her back.

I wasn't keen on the sheep fanks, I preferred my sheep covered in gravy or mint sauce!

Fishing for trout, was great fun, tickling trout, I don't recall who taught me, we used to go down to a stream at night with a torch, stand barefoot in the stream then whenever a trout came along, you shone the torch in its face and the trout would stop and stay still then you'd put your hand into the water slowly so as not to make any ripples, tickled the fish on its back and moved your hand up to behind its gills. You timed the opening of the gills, as the gills opened you shoved your thumb and first finger in and threw it to land.

When electricity first arrived on the island, although the houses had been wired, we didn't know when it would be live. Previously it had been my job to light the Tilly Lamp as it got dark. I was at a neighbour's house one day and heard it was to be turned on at 4pm that day. When I went home for my tea at six, I never let on, and as usual, we had no sooner started our tea my father said, "it is getting very dark, better put the Tilly on Callum". I stood up as if to get the Tilly lamp, but instead switched on the light, my father and mother jumped out of their chairs with fright. I was always keen on reading books, and that allowed me to read while I was in bed. Eventually my mother would shout, "put that light out", after that I brought a torch with me, and read under the covers. Whilst at secondary school, which was not so bad, we had fun with the girls, it wasn't that I was chasing the girls, because they would pelt me with sticks and stones if I stepped out of line. We had our share of bullies, but we had our ways of dealing with them. We experimented with smoking and drinking, and some of us got hooked, I only stopped smoking fifteen years ago after a lifetime of smoking and drinking. I still enjoy a wee tipple or two. These habits cost money and so we did a few jobs around the village like cutting the grass for someone or bringing in the peats. We would also collect lemonade bottles and beer bottles that were thrown into the drains, by adults returning home on Friday and Saturday nights.

Cutting and bringing home the peats was another chore we had to do, that would be done with big tractors, and almost every day a tractor would be sinking on the moor often with a trailer load of peats. On one occasion a tractor went down in a bog and as they tried to get it out it dug itself in deeper, even with two further tractors pulling it kept going down, at the end of the day they gave up. Because the exhaust was two feet vertical on the engine, fearing that it would sink deeper, they stuck a tree branch into it. Returning the following day with two tracked tractors, they dug it out, all you could see was the top of the tree branch. It took them three days, but they managed it.

The dances at the weekend were great fun, we used to have one in the local hall every so often. The hall was constructed of wood, with a wooden floor, and as you went through the door you had to time yourself with the music, because with everybody dancing the floor was bouncing up and down at least six to eight inches. If you mistimed it, you fell flat on your face. I have a photo of my sister with a fellow from the village, they were dancing, he with his with his wellies on as he had come straight from the moor, we would have a right horro yally.

One Friday night a crowd of us went down to the Keose road end, the local girls were to meet us there, someone had taken an accordion with him, but could only play a few tunes. He began playing, and next thing some were dancing. As the cars came back from their Friday night sessions most of them stopped and joined in. It was hilarious as some of them could hardly stand never mind dance. Town hall dances started about nine when the pubs closed and finished at midnight, and then you were off to the country dances. There would always be fights at the town hall. One local legend, though I didn't witness it became common knowledge at the time. A fellow from the town came to the dance as he was emigrating to Canada in the morning, three guys picked a fight with him, and the fighting eventually spilled out of the side door onto Point St. An elderly lady walking by spotted a police car parked close by, she approached them to ask if they could stop the fighting, as he seemed to be on his own. The policeman said, he is doing OK on his own, they are getting what they deserve. He put the three guys in hospital, each with a broken nose and other bruises, and went on the boat in the morning and on to Canada. There was always rivalry between the town boys and the country lads. I am glad to say I was never involved in any.

I recall one Friday leaving the town hall, there were four of us. I had my own car by then, going to a dance in Ness, twenty-five to thirty miles away. When we arrived, there were only six to eight people there. Someone mentioned that there was a dance in Harris, so off we went, mad or not. Harris was at least sixty miles away, and we arrived sometime after two in the morning, that was a good night out. Until I remembered that I had to work in the morning, I managed to get there just five minutes late. Whenever we went to town, we used to look out for the lorries going to the gutting factory, they were full of Mackerel to be made into fish meal, the lorries were so overloaded that the fish were sliding off and landing on the road. we would run along behind filling bags with Mackerel, if we didn't keep them for ourselves, we would deliver them to local families who needed them.

3 My Teens

When I left secondary school, I attended the castle school to begin learning a trade. Our choices were Engineering, Textiles, Navigation, or construction, I chose construction. For some reason I began in the second year, which meant I was the youngest in the class. One of our teachers must have hated me, he taught the last four periods on Friday. First day he asked me a question, and I did not have a clue what he was talking about, I think it was something they had covered the previous year. Well, I got a rollicking, the following Friday same thing happened, so I thought to myself, I've had enough of this. The following Friday, after roll call, which came after lunch, me and one or two others skived off into town. We played cards and drank coffee in the local cafe. We had fun with the teachers as well, some of the classes were taken in a wooden hut among the trees, and the teacher was always late, so instead of lining up at the door, we climbed the trees, and waited till he arrived. He couldn't see us so he shouted for us to come, then we would get a rollicking.

P.T. was murder, we had to strip down to our shorts, then off for a two-mile run through the castle grounds, it didn't matter if it was raining, snowing, or blowing a gale, no excuses. The principal used to ask for two volunteers to go down for a bucket of coal for the fire, the coal was stored in the cellar so you had to go down the stairs and then drag a big bucket of coal up the steps, and nobody would volunteer. Then, one day, he picked me and another pupil to go for the coal, the principal was a keen fisherman, and we were admiring all the rods and waders he had. Then for a laugh, the other chap started to pull on the waders but couldn't get them on. We looked inside and pulled out a half bottle of whisky. I don't know long it took us to get that bucket into the classroom, but by the time we arrived we were well shot, and he was giving us some strange looks. After that, there was no shortage of volunteers, we found out later that he was an alcoholic, and hid bottles all over the place.

One Saturday afternoon while sitting in a chair, trying to catch up on some sleep, I felt my shoulder being shaken. I woke up with a start and found a policeman standing beside me, my first thoughts were, crikey! what did I do. Our front door was open, and he got no answer when he shouted so he walked in and saw me asleep luckily, he just wanted to speak to my father, so I went to fetch him from the loom shed. The policeman handed him a wee purse with a silver sixpence inside and asked him did he recognize it. My father couldn't remember ever seeing it before, the policeman explained that they were in the process of moving stations from Kenneth Street to Church Street. where it is to this day. Someone had found the purse in the back of a drawer, they searched through their records, and discovered that my father had found it on the street, then handed it in to the police. My father had forgotten all about it, that was in 1915 or 1920, that sixpence was a week's wage back then. After leaving the Castle I was at home unemployed for nearly a year, but eventually got a job as an apprentice joiner with a local builder. As I had no car or driving licence at that time, I had to rely on lifts to work and back again, that carried on for a year until I decided it would be best if I lodge in town. I stayed with a nice family, after a while the landlady's son decided I should be introduced to a pub. He took me to the back room of the Calley bar, that was the start of my going into pubs. I mentioned earlier about the fights in the town hall, I was never involved with any of them, but I did have a fight with a fellow from the next village. I had been in bed for three days with the flu, or a similar virus, I went out to the hall and was playing darts with someone, when a crowd of boys from the next village came in. I could see one of them was looking for a fight, he was known for fighting at the dances. He later admitted that was the only reason he went, as I had never seen him on the dance floor. He accused me of constantly going to their village, to bothering their girls. I tried to tell him that I was in bed for the last three days, and had been nowhere near them, that did not sink in, and he kept on accusing me. well, being accused of something I hadn't done annoyed me, so after about half an hour of pushing and shoving I said I wouldn't fight him in the hall, it would have to be outside, so off we went. I still tried to reason with him, until he tried to land one on me and that clinched it. I managed to dodge his blow and I threw a punch, which landed, and drew blood. We fought for a wee while, then Doyan, who oversaw the hall, separated us. He gave us a talking to, I am proud to say, I came out of that scrape intact. The next time we came across each other was about a month later, I went into the Crown inn for a drink after work, after placing my order, the barman came with my drink and said it was paid for, looking around to see who had paid for it, I saw Kenny at the end of the bar, we have been friends ever since.

My first pet was my father's sheep dog, if she was not working the sheep, she would be with me. she was brought up with me, her name was Wallace. One night my uncle called in to tell my father he had to put his own dog to sleep for some reason. My father offered him Wallace, as he had another dog, a sad day for me, as she was brought up with me, and was a lovely pet. Three days later my uncle got in touch to tell us that Wallace had disappeared, could we look out for her in case she came back to us. She was kept on a lead for two nights, and the third night he thought she would be OK, and he let her out, that was the last time he saw her. A week later we heard that a woman over on the west side who was calling her husband in for tea. Her husband's name was Wallace, and as soon as she shouted his name the dog came running up to her, they decided to keep her and left word with my father. I had other pets too, I had a rabbit for two years, I used to take it out on a lead until one day, I went out to feed it and found it dead.

I used to go down to the shore to pick mussels, if I saw an eel, I would catch it with a jam jar and take it home. They wouldn't survive for long as I didn't know how to feed them. When we were first married, we had Honey a small dog of mixed breed, then Bouncer another black mixed breed, she was brilliant at football, would have put Pele to shame. I took her over to the park one day and there was a crowd playing football, as I let her off the lead, she was away, after the ball, and nobody was taking it away. A couple of tourists sitting on a bench laughed their heads off watching us, try to get either the dog or the ball. After a while, we got Bouncer a friend, a Samoyed called Laski, the two of them had great fun chasing each other from the kitchen into the living room and out again. Sadly, Bouncer eventually passed away. One day, out on the moor to lift the peats, I had Laski with me, we had no sooner arrived when Laski spotted some sheep, he took off to play with them. If anybody had seen us, I would have been shot as well as Laski. The last dog we had was Molly, we had her for several years, until she passed away after a good life, only a dog, some might say, but each one was a part of our family. We had a cat called Smoky, when we went on holiday to Ireland, we left food at one of our neighbours, when we got back our neighbour told us that she had not seen Smoky since the day we left, that had been three weeks before. when I got up the following morning, Smoky was sitting on the front step when I opened the door.

I was always keen on gardening and decided one year to plant a bag of potatoes on my father's croft, however finding time to tend to them as they were growing was another thing. I was very often working until late at night, I remember cleaning and hoeing them at eleven thirty-one night, but to no avail, as when the time came to lift them, I only got one bag. That didn't put me off growing vegetables in the garden. I had success, at all the houses we lived in. Until we came to the house we are in at the moment, although the ground was not that great for vegetables, I had some success, until one night after coming home at nine at night and going out to see to them, having not seeing to them for three nights, the turnips that I was about to lift had been eaten by slugs. well after that I had to give something up either my vegetables or my jobbing, the jobs won.

I remember when our youngest son was taken to hospital to have his appendix removed, they were about to burst. After that our two youngest were sent to Raigmore, the nearest general hospital, on the mainland, in Inverness. They needed to have their tonsils and adenoids removed, they were always getting sore throats. It was decided that they would be operated on at the same time, rather than separately. One New Year's Day I shall always remember, our younger daughter started to complain about earache, and that was the only time the doctor was off. About an hour later her face started to swell and there was no way to take her to hospital. I phoned the doctors surgery but was told it was his day off, however, he was driving to Harris at that time he would stop off to see her, as he was passing. By the time he arrived she was screaming and hitting her head on the floor with pain and her ear had practically disappeared into the swelling. The doctor gave her an injection of something and that seemed to stop the swelling. He said he didn't know what the cause was and told us to prepare to fly her out to Raigmore. He was dropping his wife off in Tarbert and he would call in on the way back and decide then. When he arrived back, an hour later, the swelling had gone down. he gave her another injection, then stayed with us for an hour, to see how she responded. As he left, he told us if it happened again to ring him, I am glad to say it didn't, we still don't know what the cause was.

Another time, I was invited to a wedding dance in the town hall, as most of my mates were going, I thought why not? At the dance, I noticed some people going out to the back door, then returning with half pints. Curiosity got the better of me and I went to see what was going on, there were two big kegs of beer. while I was taking all this in, someone asked if I was dancing, no, I replied. If I was, it wouldn't be with him. "Alright, it's your turn on the keg", he said, he had to show me what to do, as I had never seen one before. It was quite busy, so when things slackened off, I thought to myself, this must be good stuff, and poured myself a half pint, then another. Well, by the end of the night I was singing glory, glory, hallelujah. I had to be taken back to my digs at the end of the night, no way could I walk home, to make matters worse, they had to wake up my landlady, boy did I get a rollicking. I was there for about a year, then decided to leave as I was not saving any money. I was back to thumbing a lift again. I was able to get overtime three nights a week until nine o'clock so decided to save up, buy myself a van, and learn to drive. Otherwise, getting home at night meant taking the bus, for the first seven miles, and then walking the other five. Walking home at night when it was very dark was creepy, you couldn't see your hand in front of your face, the only way I knew I was still on the road, was when I could feel the stone chips under my feet. I was often given a lift. I remember one night walking home, it was so dark that I couldn't see anything, then I saw the light of the lodge, after coming round the Soval bends, and I knew where I was. Farther on I noticed another light and thought, that can't be there, then it disappeared, I couldn't understand which light it could be, then, the light came into view again. I was so scared, all sorts of things went through my mind, was it a ghost? was it the banshee? I carried on walking, looking over my shoulder every wee while, the light kept blinking on and off, then it stopped. I kept looking behind me until that light came on only ten yards behind me. It was a young couple smooching in a car, the light I was seeing was the internal light of the car. I had walked right past the car, but never saw or heard a thing, I don't know who would have got the biggest fright if we had spotted each other.

When I was about fourteen, Hector and I started experimenting with cigarettes, we were always trying to find a quiet spot to have a quick smoke. The best place was the outside toilet, that was a shed built onto the end of the byre. It had a toilet in one end and some hay for the cow at the other end, there was also a can of fuel for the outboard, a lethal combination. We had no sooner lit our cigarettes than the hay burst into flames, we tried to beat it out but to no avail. We decided that the best thing to do was scarper. So, we ran around to the other end, then turned around and walked back as if nothing had happened. We met my brother coming towards us shouting, he had been upstairs shaving and had seen the smoke, he had shaved one side of his face and still had the foam on the other side. There was nothing we could do but watch, then the next thing Boom, the roof went up in the air. My father had to put a new roof on the following day and go to town for a new toilet. I think we had the inside toilet shortly after that, as I remember watching my father shuttering the walls.

Another job I had to do was the bobbins for my father, as he was a weaver as well as a crofter. I tried to dodge it if I could, I would rather go out with my mates, or into town. One Christmas eve I managed to dodge it, or deliberately forgot, and went off to town. When I came back, before going to bed I hung my socks above the fire. When I came down in the morning, I saw my two socks bulging above the fireplace with an orange sticking out of the top of one, good, Santa remembered me. When I took the orange out, I looked to see what else was there, empty bobbins in both, that was my lot, and a reminder that I still had to do the bobbins for him, no getting away with it?

Another time, when I was in my teens, I was walking home alone. The night was pitch black, and I could hardly see a thing, I was guided by the telegraph poles as I could see the tops of them. I could hear a noise but couldn't understand what it was. There was a swish swish, it went on for a while and every time I stopped the noise stopped, it was baffling me, and every time I started walking that noise started again. I stopped and said, "who is that"? A woman screamed right beside me, I nearly had a heart attack, she had been walking beside me all the way, and neither of us knew. She was wearing a light oilskin coat and Wellington boots as it had been raining earlier, the oilskin was rubbing on her boots which made the noise, she was so close that she could hear my footsteps.

Another job I had to do was threshing the corn. My father had a wee mill to thresh the corn, it consisted of what looked like a forty-five-gallon drum with nails sticking out of it, within a wooden cage and powered by wooden pedals. To work it you sat on a high seat, and peddled away, as you pushed the corn in, it came out the other side, leaving the seed in a tray underneath. I wanted to go into town that night as it was a Friday, so I thought if I peddled fast enough, I could lift my feet up, and push the corn through. As I took my feet off the peddles, there was an almighty explosion. I found myself on the floor, the drum took off and hit the back wall of the byre, then burst in two, the wooden sides flew sideways and something else went through the window, other bits hit the roof. I picked myself up and walked out of the byre, to see my father and a neighbour running around like mad, trying to work out what had happened. I'm not sure if I made it to town that night, after that I had to do it by hand, It could only happen to me. My father used to have corn stacks as well as haystacks, we used to have great fun when the corn stacks were put in the byre. When we got down to the last couple of dozen sheaves, we used to get the dogs and the cats around us, and buckets of water, as underneath the stack would be mice and rats in their holes. When you poured the water down the holes the rats would come up half drowned then the cats and dogs were after them.

The first van that I bought was a green A35 Austin. I had never sat in the driver's seat with the engine running, so on the way home with the van, the fellow I bought it from was showing me how everything worked. I soon got the hang of things and passed my test first time. On the day of the test when the examiner asked me to do an emergency stop, he nearly went through the windscreen as safety belts were not yet required. My eldest brother had the test after me, when he finished, I asked him how he had got on, "no bother" he said, "I failed".

I was at work one day when the police came looking for me, I thought to myself, what have I done now. They asked when I had gotten the van.? Who from? Who had it last, was I ever on the mainland with it? all kinds of questions. I asked what all this was about, they said someone had been killed in the south of England in a hit and run, and the only details they had was a green a35 van was involved. Having my own transport helped a lot, like going to and from work, and doing jobs on the side, they did not help me financially, as all the jobs I got were for friends and relatives, and I would end up having to pay for materials myself, finishing up with a loss. It was handy on Friday and Saturday nights, we could go whenever we wanted to go, instead of relying on buses, which was great. The next car I had was a fiat 500, a small car with the engine at the back. I was never off the road then, there was one time, I was at a dance in Ness, and I was dropping off a friend in Shawbost, on the way home, in the early hours of the morning. I don't remember driving on the Achmore road, but when I came to the main road to Harris, I had to break hard, as I was about to shoot off the road. I realised that I had been nodding off, so I pulled in at the Leurbost crossroads, switched of the engine, folded my seat back, and went to sleep. I wasn't asleep for long as I felt myself rocking and shaking, I sat up with a start, saw that I had not pulled on the hand break, or left it in gear and it was moving. The two left wheels were in the drain with the right wheels on the road. I had travelled about twenty yards and was heading for the river just yards away. I was suddenly wide awake, I managed to get onto the road and drive home. I had that car for about two or three years, until one night, on the way home from Stornoway, I hit a patch of ice just as I was coming onto the Mary bank bridge, I didn't stand a chance, as I hit the parapet the front crumbled, as the engine was in the back, and the steering wheel came up and broke my jaw. When I regained consciousness, two young girls were looking in the window at me, next an ambulance took me to hospital. I was then flown to Bangour hospital, between Glasgow and Edinburgh. I had sixty stitches in my jaw and some skin grafted, and was fed on liquids, as the only way I could open my mouth, was keeping it open with my finger, and putting in a straw. After a fortnight recuperating in Glasgow, and attending the Glasgow Royal, that kept me quiet for some time. I remember missing the New Year celebrations that year. As the Fiat was a right off, I then bought a van, a Grey Morris minor which I shared with my brother. If he wanted to go out drinking, he would give me the keys, and vise-versa. I was soon back up to my old shenanigans. I went into town one Saturday for some messages and parked in the car park, when I came back, I jumped into the van and started reversing back, I found the clutch a bit sharp but didn't think much of it. As I drove to the exit and braked, I knew something was wrong. I looked behind me, there was a seat in the back, I didn't have a seat in mine. I had the wrong van, Grey Morris vans were very common, what do I do now I could not reverse back there was a car behind me wanting out, nothing for it I had to carry on into the traffic and hope the driver would not come back looking for his van, also hoping the parking space was still there when I came back in, lucky for me the parking spot was still there. I felt stupid coming out of one van and jumping into another and driving off, often the same ignition key could operate similar vans and cars. One night driving back from a dance, about five miles from home, the van started giving me trouble, and overheating, I stopped to see what the problem was, opening the bonnet I found that I had a broken fan belt, so we had to either walk home, or sleep in the van and wait till morning to get a lift. well neither was an option as it was about 3am. I turned to my female companion and asked her to take her tights off, there was a firm no, there would be no prospect of that, or of anything else for that matter. Finally, when I explained why I wanted them, she agreed if I bought new ones the following day, that was OK. I turned my back for her privacy turning the tights into a sort of rope, she looked on in bewilderment, as I wrapped it round the fan to act as a belt. I filled the radiator with water, by that time it had cooled down, so off we went, that took us home and took me to town the following day. You should have seen the mechanics face when he saw it, he could not stop laughing.

New Year parties were great, as soon as New Year came in, we were off round the village, wishing everyone a happy new year. Sometimes we didn't get home until three days later. On one occasion I was at a party, it was about three am, the lady of the house started cooking salt herring and potatoes that made us thirstier and made us drink even more. One party I shall never forget, it was hilarious, someone had felt sick and went outside, when we were going home at about six in the morning, there were about half a dozen hens on the path, standing on one leg and toppling over. We couldn't stop laughing, Wherever the guy had vomited, the hens had found it and got drunk. When you see a drunken hen, you will laugh.

4 London Bound

Once I had completed my five-year joinery apprenticeship for a while I was employed by the same company. I didn't want to be working for the same firm all my life, I wanted to see the world, or at least part of it. I read about Australia and the assisted passages there, you could get to Australia from London for ten pounds, however if you returned within two years you had to pay the full return fare. I read all I could about it, found out they were desperate for joiners, and that was it, I was ready for the off. I had to have a full medical which was done in Stornoway by a doctor appointed by them, I passed that, and was told that I was sponsored by Sydney Rotary club. They organised to pick me up from the airport and had a place for me to stay and a job to start. Once I was settled in great, all this had taken months to organize. Then I had a letter with an appointment at Australia house in London and I was to wait for the date of my departure flight. My father didn't mind me going, but my mother was not too happy, any way I said my good- byes and off I went. I had been to London before, at my sister's wedding so I knew what to expect. I remember on that occasion we were shown the sights of London the day before the wedding, I don't know who by, but I was walking behind my brother, hanging on to his jacket with my hand on my wallet, going along Petticoat Lane, which was a massive outdoor market. I could see a man carrying a placard heading towards me, it seemed to take ages, finally I could read what was on it THE END IS NYE. Thank goodness I thought, the sooner we get out of here the better, as he passed by, I looked at the other side and it read, YOU HAVE BEEN WARNED. Going to the interview at Australia house, was the start of one of my hilarious episodes in life. Standing in front of the multi-story block of offices, I thought what have I let myself in for, well here goes, so I entered the building and followed the crowd. Just my luck, my appointment was on the top floor, I followed the others until eventually I found the right office. I had my interview, and left, that went OK, good. I discovered that there was a lift, I patiently waited for it, hoping that somebody would come along, and I could follow them, as I had never been in a lift before, nobody did. Eventually the lift arrived, and the doors opened, as I stepped in, I looked at the panel and pressed B, good I thought this is simple enough, Bottom. When I stepped out, I realized the B I had pressed had meant basement. I found myself in the basement, among a pile of rubbish and machinery. Crikey!! How do I get out of this. ?? as I pressed the buttons nothing seemed to work everybody seemed to go to the top floor, it always came down to no1 and then off up to the top floor, Panic stations. I kept thinking of the headlines in the Stornoway Gazette, Lewis man found starved to death in basement of Australia House. Well, I think that lift took hours to get back down to the basement, was I glad to see daylight, when it eventually arrived. Come to think of it I never thought at the time that there must be stairs I could use. While waiting for my flight to Australia I applied for a job as a joiner in a shop fitting factory, that was good, the interview went OK, and I got the job. The following Monday as I went on the train and tube to work, I couldn't see anybody on the tube with working clothes like me, full bib and brace, everybody else seemed to be in collar and tie, then getting off the bus everyone wore black suits, bowler hats and brolly, swinging a briefcase. What kind of place was I going into? must be posh, as I followed them into the canteen, what I saw made me laugh to myself, as each man came in, he placed his briefcase on the table, bowler hat and brolly on the coat hook, opened his briefcase, took his lunch box out and set it aside then out came the overalls. Vain or not? I was the only Scot on the job the foreman was English the rest were Europeans, two Pakistanis, a Cypriot, Nigerians, West Africans, it was like the league of nations. It was there I noticed the Pakistanis used their saw upside down and cut on the up stroke from underneath. Coming up to Christmas, work was quiet, as the shops did not want their customers inconvenienced. We still had to stand by our benches, in case a rush job came in. As the English celebrated Christmas and the Scots new year, the thought of working over new year did not appeal to me, so I quit the job and returned home. I had abandoned my plan to go to Australia, a decision I regret to this day. A fortnight at home was OK, and then it was back down to London. In London, as we walked to work, we would buy a newspaper to read on the way, very few shops were open at that time in the morning, but the newspapers would be piled on boxes on street corners, with an honesty box beside them, I am sure they made more money that way than selling them in the shop, as some mornings I would see ten shilling notes, even pound notes, and the paper only cost about sixpence; that soon stopped when the drug addicts came on the scene, and knew they were on to a good thing. Taking the train from Glasgow at midnight arriving at kings cross at six in the morning, it was very easy to get a job in those days. The daily papers would have four pages of jobs to choose from, I had a job within a half hour, often before leaving the station. I once had a job working on a convent in Roehampton in South London, that was a laugh and a half, every door you went through had a small container of holy water, hanging to one side of it. which the nuns used to dip their fingers in and cross themselves. well, every door I came through, that container went toppling to the floor, then a mad rush to find a tap and fill it with water before the nuns saw you, it always happened to me. I met a nice novice nun there, she seemed to take a shine to me as she always seemed to look out for me for a chat. I tried to convince her to change her profession, but didn't have any luck, but we parted on good terms. We used to frequent a pub near the mall called the clachan bar, all the highland folk used to go there at weekends. if you saw a crowd of girls at a table you knew there was a party going somewhere, so we would go and chat them up to get an invite. A policeman who used to come in after his shift, he was from Harris, he used to shove his uniform jacket and hat under my seat, and say," look after that". We were in his car one night going to a party, and he had a few in him, driving down the mall towards a set of traffic lights, he ran into the car in front. As quick as a flash, he jumped out and shouted to the other driver to keep his handbrake on, as he had broken his sidelight. The other driver must have had even more to drink, he didn't realize that he couldn't roll backwards uphill. He apologized and handed him £30 for the broken light, then shot off. The policeman got back into the car and said we can get a good carry out with this, then drove on.

I was walking to work one morning, when I felt my collar being grabbed, the next thing I knew a big police car skidded to a halt beside me, and whoever had my collar opened the back door and threw me in, by the time I found my bearings and worked out what had happened the car had driven off. It was the policeman from Harris, I thought I was being abducted, he just laughed and took me to work. One day, on my way to work, rushing to catch the tube, as I raced down the stairs to the platform, two guys were passing by, when one of them asked the other a question in Gaelic, and I answered in Gaelic, and carried on. As I jumped on the tube, I turned around they were looking after me wondering who I was, to this day I don't know who they were. By this time, I had met Kenny, from Harris, he was a right character, and we had some comical times together. We moved into a flat together, he found one in North London, there was a pub across the road, which was handy. It had two single beds, fridge, wardrobe, cooker, sink, and a gas fire with two chairs, that was all we needed. We fed the gas meter with the same sixpence the entire time we were there, we would put it in the top and hold your hand under the meter to catch it as it came out, nothing to do with us, it was like that when we went in. One Saturday, someone knocked on the door, Kenny thought it was for the rent, as he hadn't told them I was staying with him he told me to hide.

There was nowhere to hide, the only place was an empty wardrobe, but when I jumped in, the doors kept swinging open, so Kenny had to stand in front and keep them closed. It turned out to be the gas man, who gave him a telling off when there was no money in the box, and a queer look as he passed the wardrobe, as the doors started to swing open, Kenny would dive to keep them closed.

Kenny had been working in Ayr the previous year, he was a plumber. He had an accident in the works van while going to work after a party, he had knocked over a motorcyclist at a Junction, he was charged but never heard anything about a court case, so he travelled down to London. I was sitting in the flat one night reading a book, when a knock came to the door. I went to answer it, two guys stood there, and they asked for Kenny, I told them he was not back from work yet, so they said, to tell him Jim and Iain looked in to see him. OK I said, and they left. I told Kenny when he came in, but he hadn't a clue who they were, so he jumped into bed, dressed just as he had been when he finished working on the drain. No sooner had he fallen asleep than the door went again, I answered and the two guys from earlier, barged past me. one stood at the end of the bed and the other at the side, they woke him up. Kenny ----------- you are under arrest, get your clothes on, we are on the midnight flight up to Edinburgh. Well, that was hilarious, he turned to them and said, "ah well I was always wondering when you would come and collect me", then panic stations he did not have a clean shirt or a tie, he had to borrow mine, then off he went in handcuffs. We were very friendly with the landlord of the pub, across the road and had a phone call from Kenny, asking if he would pay his fine and his fare down to London, which he did, he was working nights behind the bar for the next six months. It was in that pub that I possibly came across the notorious murderer Dennis Neilson, who lived next door to us. Although I can't remember meeting him, we were always passing the time of day with others. I only realized this when I saw it on the news years later. That is my claim to fame. Another time, I arranged to meet someone in a certain pub, as I entered, I noticed a woman she was back and forth from the one-armed bandit machine, putting money in, now and again she would go and sit at the table with her friends to have a drink.

However, she kept returning to put more money in. Sometimes wining a few shillings, but not often. I had just got myself a drink and was given sixpence change, instead of putting it into my pocket I leaned over slightly and put it in the machine as the woman had just left and gone to her table. I just pulled the lever and out came the jackpot, well if looks could kill, I would have been dead by now. When my companion came in, I bought him a drink and we both left. The woman looked like a pensioner and had probably put all her money into that machine, it was just the luck of the draw.

My sister was living in Richmond at the time and had invited me over for Sunday dinner. The bus terminal was just outside the pub door, and I could see when it was leaving, but you had time to down your drink. One Sunday, waiting in the pub for the bus to leave, I saw the driver getting on, that was it, down with my drink and step on it, up the stairs to the top deck, and took the front seat, so that I could see the sights. It was about half an hour's drive to Richmond, that was half past twelve, just in time for my dinner at one o'clock. Sometime later, I woke up and looked at my watch 7pm, confused and unable to figure out where I was, then I realized I was on a bus as the lights had been dimmed but the bus was at a standstill. Looking out the window all I could see were trees and streetlights, it was dark. then I remembered getting on the bus and going for my Sunday dinner. I stood up walked downstairs and found the driver asleep on the back seat, the conductor was stretched out reading the paper. He sat up with a start and asked where in heavens name, I had come from, and where had I got on. He could not believe it when I told him I had got on at Hornsey Rise, he said that the bus had been re- routed twice since then, and we were now in the south of Surrey. He told me to walk back about a hundred yards, and get a bus into the train station, that was it, train back into London and then the tube, then bus again. I walked into the flat at about 10 pm. starving. I never did get my Sunday lunch. only a rollicking from my sister. My sister asked if I would baby sit for them as they wanted to go out to a film or pub or something, so I said OK, go and enjoy yourselves. The kids were very young at the time, I'm not sure if they were in school or not. I managed to put them down in their cots, and I went to watch a film. Sometime later I woke up and went to check on them, my nephew was sitting up in his cot reading a book, and I asked him where his sister was as she wasn't in her cot, he didn't know he said. Then I heard someone talking downstairs and ran down. I found her standing on a chair trying to lift the latch on the door, and my brother in-law shouting words of encouragement through the letter box, that was another rollicking from my sister. The next time I baby sat for them they were a bit older but not much, and again I fell asleep watching a film, but this time met my sister and her husband coming in the door holding my niece's hand she had managed to open the door and crossed a main road, that was the end of my baby-sitting days. After coming from work one Friday, there was no sign of Kenny, so I went across the road to the pub. It was called the Favourite, to see if he was there, he was with another crowd, I joined them and we didn't leave until Sunday afternoon, and that was to get something to eat, as the landlady kept filling us up with sandwiches, a big tray full would be sent down in this lift from upstairs every so often. That Monday morning, I went to work with a bit of a hangover but lasted the day, I went to the station to get a ticket home, I did not have enough money on me for the ticket, what now, I couldn't walk it, I was miles away. I searched my pockets and found enough to take me on the train to Hammersmith, and then walked the two miles to my sister's place. I got another rollicking; she was not pleased. Another time in the Favourite, we had a wee party, and it was well past closing time, early hours of the morning, suddenly, this heavy knocking on the door. The landlord who had been drinking with us, leapt over the bar and said it's the police, threw a pile of aprons at us and said, quick start clearing the tables, you're all my employees, and went to open the door to let them in. Whatever story he told them, I don't recall, but I remember the police giving us some sideways glances as they left. All these episodes make you think that we did nothing but drink and party, we worked hard as well, all the drinking was done at the weekends. On one of those weekend sorties Kenny and I were walking home, and for a laugh we decided to walk up through Soho. When we were about twenty yards up the street, we were accosted by two ladies of the night, who asked us if we wanted a good time. We were careful how much money we carried with us, so we only carried around what we needed. We told them we did not have much money on us but that didn't put them off, as they proceeded to search our pockets. I think they found about four shillings between us. never mind, we could come with them anyway and have a chat, they lead us into a wee flat, where, sitting in an armchair was an old woman busy knitting, another young girl, and on the settee a young fellow who seemed the worse for drink, as he was fast asleep. we had hardly sat down when there was a heavy knocking on the door. The old woman whispered to the others, "that's the police", turned to us and said "I am Morag you are friends of mine and have come to visit", by that time one of the girls we had gone in with, had run over to the wall, opened a hatch in the ceiling which was papered over, jumped on the other ones back and pulled herself up, she then proceeded to pull her friend up with her. Well, I can`t describe what I saw as her naked backside disappeared into the loft. The hatch closed just before the police came in, they shook the young fellow awake and pointed him to the door. They asked who we were, and as I was going to say friends of Morag, he just pointed to the door, and out we went. Just as we were going one of the officers asked where the other two girls were. After running down the street, we waited at the corner to see what would happen, ten minutes later the police came out with the girls in handcuffs, and that was us off home. Another time walking home late at night, the buses had stopped and, you couldn't get a taxi at that time of night as they were all finished for the night. I asked a taxi driver if he could take me to Hammersmith, he said he was not for hire, but I could sit in the luggage rack as he was going in that direction. It was one of the black cabs with the luggage rack where the passenger seat would be, with no door. well, that was OK, except every time he turned to the right, I was hanging on for dear life to stop myself being flung out onto the road and meet my maker. I finally arrived and once he stopped at the traffic lights, shouted my thanks, and jumped off.

One day, Kenny, another guy and me were sitting in the flat, at a loose end, when we remembered meeting three guys from Stornoway. A few weeks before. They had given us their address, so we decided to go and visit them. When we reached their street, we looked for the number they had given us. It was a big two-story house which was often rented out to lodgers, it was in a nice area to, so we thought how lucky they were. We knocked on the door, no answer, tried the door, it was open, so in we went, shouting their names still no answer. From the front door you could see into the kitchen and on the table was a bottle of whisky and six cans of beer. Well, they wouldn't mind us having a drink surely, so we looked around, found some glasses, and poured ourselves a large one and opened a can each, we would re- reimburse them later. We waited there yarning, thinking that they were probably at the supermarket and would not be long. Once the beer cans were empty, and the bottle was nearly empty too, we decided to go to the local supermarket to see if we could find them. We stood in the hallway admiring the décor, when we noticed three police helmets on the hall table, and three Police jackets hanging on hooks behind the door. we glanced at each other, I think we all had the same thought, I don't think that Mo Farah would have kept up with us as we ran for our lives. When We met the Stornoway boys later, they told us that they had moved out the week before, because it was too expensive. Our flat was very near the Hammersmith Pallais and there was always something on, especially at weekends. I used to go there on a Friday evening, for the dancing. There was a bar at one end with soft drinks at the other end upstairs, and you could see down onto the dance floor. Once I topped up on Dutch courage, I would go down to see if there might be anybody I knew. The girls used to sit along the side of the hall, with the boys standing in front of them. I walked along when a lovely looking girl in the second row caught my eye, I went over and asked her for a dance. The music was so loud, she just nodded, and held her hand for me to lead her onto the dance floor. When I turned to dance with her, I nearly fainted, she was about three feet tall, and only reached just above my waist. It turned out that she was French, without a word of English, she must have been standing on a chair when I asked her to dance. I didn't want to embarrass her, so we had a wee dance then I made my excuses, failed again.

One morning, when I arrived for work at the convent, while sitting on a bench, I saw a squirrel. It ran down the trunk of the tree in front of me, then jumped up on the bench beside me, every time I made a move to touch or stroke him, he was off up the tree like a bullet. I fed him bits of my sandwich from my lunch box, after that, he must have been looking out for me, as soon as I arrived every morning, he was up beside me on that bench and looking up at me wanting some food. He was very cute.

When walking home late one night, a young girl approached me, asking for money. I stepped to one side to get past her, but she moved in front of me again. I could see she had taken drugs, and she had a Scottish accent. I knew that if I gave her money, it would go on drugs, so I told her that I wouldn't give her money but as we were outside a late-night café, I would buy her a meal. We went into the cafe, and I ordered her a full breakfast, Bacon, egg, and sausages all the trimmings, I ordered a cup of tea for myself. She was so young, I knew she must have run away from home, so I tried to get her to talk about herself, but she wouldn't. When we left the café, she went one way and I the other, never to meet again.

On one of my frequent Friday night visits to the Palais, and as usual drinking more than I should, I found myself walking down the middle of the road following the white centre line. A taxi came up behind me and I flagged it down, jumped in and told him to take me to Hammersmith, he turned round to me and said, "that's in London". "Yes", I said "where are we"? "You are on the other side of Middlesex". How I got there I have not the faintest idea. I Looked at my watch to see what the time was, nothing there, my watch strap had broken, or it had been stolen. I asked the driver what the time was, I can't remember what he said, but it was the early hours of the morning 3 or 4am. I must have had a face he could trust, or maybe he took pity on me, because he took me right to my door. That was at least an hour's drive if not more, the fare was my whole weeks wage, which I had safely stashed away in the flat.

In the first job, where they wore the bowler hats, we had long lunch breaks, so what better to do than play cards. That's when I got involved with poker, which I liked, as I was winning most of the time. Until one day, my luck ran out. We usually played for pennies or shillings, but if somebody thought they had a good hand, it would go up to ten shillings or a pound. On one occasion I lost most of my wages. However, the following Monday, when we played again, my luck changed, I won my wages back and the other guys too. I knew where this would lead, in the long run, so I quit poker, while I was ahead.

One of my jobs was on was a multi-storey block of flats or offices, somewhere in the city. It was very high, and when we were working on the sixth or eighth floor, if the hooter went for tea breaks, we didn't walk down the ladder, as we only had ten minutes. So, you straddled your feet around the ladder, and slipped down it, then ran along the scaffolding to the next ladder and so on, until you reached the ground. It was like bees at the honey pot. By the time you got to the shed, your tea was already poured for you. Leaving the tea shed one day I came across the general foreman giving an Australian guy a rollicking, seemingly he was the crane driver and had to climb down from the huge crane, which took the entire ten minutes. From then on, he had to take his lunch box and flask with him when he went up. There was a doctor and two nurses on the site and even if you had a splinter in your hand, you had to see the nurse, this happened to me twice. There would then be questions to answer, where did it happen? What side of the building was I on? What was I doing? Who was with me? All this as my finger was being wrapped up in a bandage, even though it wasn't bleeding. There were about fifty joiners on that site, and we were placing the windows and door frames in position. The bricklayers came next and built the walls. We could earn extra money if we did so much, this was our bonus. If our door frames weren't flush with their walls, they just kicked the door frame to line up, which lost us our bonus. Any fights or arguments and you were fired, after many complaints, forty joiners left, then there was only the foreman, me and a few others. I left the next week.

My next job was in the city centre, converting a four-storey building into a block of flats. I was now self-employed, which meant paying my own tax and National insurance. The man who employed us owned the building, and if you thought I liked my drink, this man had a crate full of bottles of whisky delivered every Monday. There were two joiners, including me, a couple of plumbers and electricians, two painters a tiler, a labourer, and a telephone engineer on that job. He had an office and bathroom built for him on the second floor, and when you went into see him about anything, he would be sitting at his desk with a half pint glass full of whisky. Whenever he went out, we used to go into his bathroom, and turn the bidet full on so that it would go about two feet into the air. Later in the day when he went into the bathroom, you could hear him cursing and swearing. The telephone engineer was an Irish man, he would wait nearby, and when the owner was on the phone, he ran down to the next floor and cut the wire, then all hell would break loose. "Where is that blasted phone guy?" He would curse and swear and call him all the names under the sun. We liked to torment the traffic wardens, we had a two-foot length of copper pipe, and we would stick some putty in the end, then from the second or third floor, aim it at their back as they passed by, they never knew where it came from. The other joiner, John, and I used to go to the local bar for our lunch, he was a Londoner a nice guy. One day we went in, and the barman asked if we would like to try the new German lager, which he had started selling. He warned us that it was strong, we said OK, and ordered a half pint each and a whisky that was great, and we had enough time for another round. We walked back to the job quite happy, commenting to each other on how good the lager was. When we got back to work, john was fitting the insulation into the bathroom walls as sound proofing, and I was fitting the bathroom cabinets and mirrors. As I picked up a mirror, to fit it on the wall, I suddenly felt dizzy and very tired, so I sat back on the bath. Our usual knocking off time was 4.30pm, the labourer had the job of opening up in the morning and locking up. While checking the site, he found John lying in the insulation, I hate to think what he looked like. He knew I hadn't left, as he had been working at the front door all day. He searched all four floors looking for me but couldn't find me, so he locked up and went home. As he lived not far away, he came back about seven at night, for another search, and eventually found me, fast asleep and snoring in the bath. That is an episode I would like to forget; we didn't try that lager again.

One Saturday afternoon I was walking to the tube station with the tiler, on the way he decided to call in at the betting shop, to place a bet. I wasn't in any hurry, so I stayed with him. I remember he put half a crown, two shillings and sixpence, on a six-horse accumulator which meant the winnings on the first horse went on the next horse and so on. By the time it reached the fourth race he had lost count of how much he could win. All the first five horses had won, I was watching him as the last race was on, and he was as white as a sheet, his horse fell halfway and that was it. As he said, "well I only lost two and six.

After one of my trips to the Clachan bar I was invited to a party in Acton. I noticed that it was getting late, and I wasn't feeling too good, so I decided to go back to my digs. I apologised to the host and made my exit, despite calls for me to stay till morning, and being asked if I knew how to get home, I headed off. This wouldn't be like walking to the next village, it was miles away and I was far from sober. As I wandered along side streets, without a clue where I was, I noticed a large black van crawling slowly past me a couple of times. On its third pass, it stopped in front of me, I looked up to see a policeman, he stepped out, and asked where I was going, where I had been. I didn't want him to go round and spoil the party, so I told him I couldn't remember which street it was on, I don't think I knew anyway. The next thing I knew he had a hold of my hand and was taking me into the van, I thought to myself, oh no, this is going to be my first night in the cells. He lifted me into the front beside him. within a couple of minutes, we came to a junction, he said, "there is a taxi jump out and stop it then get yourself off home".

Kenny and I were making our way back home one night, and we needed to find a toilet. We knew there were toilets down in the under pass, which you used to cross the road, so off we went. On our way we passed four guys on the way down the steps, then just before we turned into the toilets, we met another two. Once they were out of earshot, I said to Kenny, it's time they had a bath as they were stinking to high heaven. The words were no sooner out of my mouth, when I heard them shouting, "Drug squad, up against the wall". When we looked around, they had the four guys against the wall and were searching them, we carried on home. I thought later, if they went home like that, what did their wives or girlfriends think?

Coming back to the flat in Hammersmith from work one day I got off the tube and followed the crowd out onto the street, as I came out, I didn't recognise where I was. I went back inside to read the sign again, and sure enough, it was the correct station. Then I remembered that at the back of the station there was a flyover, and there it was, I had been using that station for at least six months, never realizing there was a third exit.

Another time, Kenny was hankering for some food from home, he must have phoned somebody in Harris. When I got home from work, I found a barrel of salted herring on the step. We had salted herring for breakfast, lunch, and tea, for weeks after that till we got sick of it

I never had a problem conversing with other nationalities, there was always some way or other to explain yourself, except one guy I met, and he was from Fyfe, every time he spoke, his false teeth went dancing in his mouth, then he would be cursing and swearing because of his accent I couldn't understand a word he said. I avoided him as much as possible in case he started a conversation.

While working in the convent, I was working up a ladder and whistling when I noticed a young fellow sweeping the floor, and realized he was whistling the same tune, which was a Gaelic tune, I climbed down the ladder to speak to him, thinking that he would be from the Highlands. It turned out that he came from Donegal and could speak Gaelic. we were getting some queer looks as we conversed in Gaelic in the corridor, there are differences between Irish and Scottish Gaelic, but we could understand each other.

While working in a factory, making furniture, my job was to clamp the edging on to the doors, everything was assembled and then placed in a large clamping machine. When you pulled the lever, the clamps would start off slowly and then they came together very fast, you had to watch where you put your hands, to avoid them getting caught. I remember a German guy started with us, he would have been about forty, with not a word of English, he worked alongside me, so that I could teach him how to work the machine. My nerves were shattered, every time he pulled the lever, I had to jump and grab his other hand, and pull it away from the clamps. Then he'd jump back and look at me with a Frank Spencer look, and say, "oh, oh". I thought to myself there will be more than, oh, oh, if your hand gets caught in there. I eventually persuaded him to put his left hand in his pocket before pulling the lever. I left that job shortly after, and often wonder if he still has all his fingers.

One time while home on holiday and fishing with my brother and brother-in-law. We spotted a v in the water, which told us there was a shoal of salmon, coming in the loch, trying to find the river. The three of us grabbed the net, and ran to the shore, then jumped into the boat, and rowed across the bay. By this time the shoal had circled out again having not found the estuary, we knew that they would try again so we waited and sure enough they came. As they entered the bay, my brother took one end of the net and jumped ashore while I started rowing to block them in. They must have sensed something was happening because all went quiet. Then the water appeared to be boiling. I was nearly thrown out of the boat as they took off, we were left with the top and bottom ropes, and a massive hole in the net. All we ended up with, was just one small salmon. Fishing was a good pastime during the holiday and one day I took the boat out to a place that I used to go with my father and knew all the good fishing areas. I had been out for an hour and all I caught I could hold in the palm of my hand. I went home disappointed as I hadn't caught anything worthwhile. I was told afterwards that the loch had been trawled by the fishing trawlers and nothing was left, (that is what I call greed). This not only destroyed the fishing grounds, but it also denied local people the chance to fish for their supper, some people relied on fishing to put food on the table.

Back to London, once again I had a job before leaving Kings Cross Station. I worked for a firm of shop fitters, the door to their workshop was on the main high street, you could see the traffic, and passing pedestrians. We had a small stove at one end, which the foreman kept going with offcuts of wood, to heat the place in the winter. It used to glow bright red with the heat coming from it, we were working in our tee shirts, with the temperature between eighty and ninety degrees while outside a blizzard would be blowing and it was minus two degrees. when anyone opened the door there were screams and shouts demanding that it be closed. It's a wonder none of us had a heart attack, with the sudden drop in temperature. I think it was there that I hurt my back. We had a contract to renovate the betting shops, which involved making big counters in the workshop, and lifting them onto the vans, and then into the shops. I was in agony one day and had to go home. Climbing onto the bus, the jolting of the ride back to the digs was murder. My doctor's surgery was just across the road from where I lived so I made an appointment to see him. He was German but had good English and was about a foot shorter than I was. He explained what was wrong, then told me to turn my back and clasp my hands behind my back, which just managed to do as I was in agony. He put his back to mine, grabbed my hands and the next thing my legs left the ground, and I felt my disc going back into place. I left the surgery as good as new, but as I crossed the road, I felt it go again. When I went back, he said he would arrange for me see a consultant at the hospital, which I did a month later. Meanwhile, I had to sleep on a hard floor, he also told me to watch my drinking, so from then on, I made sure there was a mirror in front of me whenever I had a drink. One time, as I was bending down to tie my shoelaces, as I got to get up, I realized I was stuck, lucky for me my flat mate was in, he was an Irishman named Paddy, he was later to be the best man at my wedding. I told paddy to throw me forwards, by putting his hand at the back of my neck, but first he wouldn't do it, as I was in front of the fire. Eventually, I persuaded him, then I found myself sitting on top of the gas fire, which was less painful than it had been, and my disc was back in place. On the day of my appointment, I made my way to the hospital. Following the usual X-ray and scans, I was to lie on a bed, the consultant started jabbing with a pin up one side and down the other about every inch, to see if I had any paralysis. While doing this, he asked where I was from and other details. He said the best exercise I could do was swimming, when I told him I couldn't swim he stood back in shock, he said, "are you telling me you were born and brought up on an island, and can't swim"? He was amazed, before I left, he gave me a list of exercises to do, some I do to this day if I feel my back sore.

Kenny and I were in the flat one night, trying to sleep, when we could hear that we had a visitor, the four-legged kind. The scratching kept us awake, and we knew that it was coming from underneath the sink, which was opposite his bed. Every so often, a shoe or a book were thrown at the sink, and that would keep it quiet for a few minutes, then it would start again. Finally, Kenny got up and said, I will sort you, as he picked up a packet of OMO washing powder, and poured the whole lot down the mouse hole, that silenced it until we got to sleep. The following night it started again, we were prepared this time, and had plenty of objects ready to throw, after that we bought a trap and caught it the following day, we weren't bothered again.

One Sunday, six of us gathered at our flat in Hornsey, and before going to the Favourite, which was the pub across the road from us, we decided to chip in and buy a big roast for dinner. A couple of us went to the shops and bought a large joint of meat and all the trimmings. I think there was enough for ten, as it took up most of the oven, then there was an argument as to what gas mark we should set it at, and for how long. Whatever was decided, we left and had a good time in the pub. When we got back to the flat hours later, starving and anticipating a lovely plate of meat and potatoes with all the veg, you can only imagine the argument blaming each other, when we opened the oven door, and saw a burnt offering, about the size of a packet of cigarettes. It was fish and chips all round.

You might think that with all the jobs I had, I was being sacked, but I was never paid off from any job, and always left either for New Year, or the summer holidays. There were plenty of jobs, you could pick and choose where to go, one of those jobs, I stayed just one week because I was staying in a flat in North London, the job involved , getting up at 5.30 am making breakfast, then catching the first bus and first tube to take me to Kings Cross Station, then catch the train down to Surrey, where I would meet the rest of the work force. The job was fitting treble glazing in private houses all over London and the outskirts, one day we went to Swansea, I think that was the only time I was in Wales. Often, we would work until six or seven pm and by the time we arrived back at the depot in Surrey, sometimes it was half past ten or eleven pm. We then had a mad rush to catch the train, the last tube and bus, twice I missed the last bus. Then I had to walk the last two miles to the flat, arriving at 2.30 or 3am, get something to eat and then bed, up again at 5.30 am. I wasn't willing to kill myself for any amount of money, so once I got my first wage, I said cheerio and left.

Working in some of those houses was a nightmare, some of them had cream or white carpets, if you stood on them, you left a mark. I am sure they even ironed the bed sheets while they were on the bed. Before you went into the house, you had to take your shoes off, and put on slippers which you were supplied with, then fit dust sheets from the front door to whichever part of the house you worked in. often the bedrooms upstairs, every time you went to get something from the van, you had to stop at the door, take your slippers off, put them in your pocket to keep them clean, and put your shoes back on, after getting what you needed, back to the door, shoes off and slippers on. When coming home on the bus, you would wait for ages, and then three or four would come at once. I would jump on the first one, no sooner had you sat down, than it would get stuck in traffic, and the other buses would overtake, sometimes, if it stopped at lights, you got off and ran after the other bus and jumped on, only to find your first bus passing you, that happened several times, very frustrating.

5 Marriage and Beyond

It was on one of my many visits to the Hammersmith Palais that I met my future wife, Valerie. We had met previously, and she had given me her telephone number, but I'd lost it. I took her home that night, and that was the beginning of our courtship. She had been in the Wrens but had then left and was working as a children's nanny. We used to go either to the dances or the pictures, usually to see whichever new film that had just been released. Valerie and I had a short engagement then got married in a Richmond Registry Office. For our honeymoon we took a couple of days in a hotel in the city and went sightseeing around London. I remember getting out of the taxi after our marriage, then going into the hotel leaving a trail of rice behind me, it kept spilling out of my case all the way to our room. My brother-in-law was the culprit, how he did it I don't know, but that rice kept coming, and showed everyone where the married couple were staying. I call her my first wife, it's not that I was married before, it just keeps her on her toes. One of the pubs I used to take her to, was near Richmond, and had two big pillars in front of the bar, and on all four sides, from about knee high up to above head height, it had the name of every whisky, beer, wine, and lager in the world. It was said, you could ask for any of them and they had it in the cellar, one of the barmen was constantly up and down from that cellar. At this time, we lived separately, so when I took her home, I still had a few miles to go, to get to my own digs, so I would thumb a lift. The taxis had all stopped running by that time, often it would be a police patrol car that would crawl by, giving me the once over. One time a van stopped and gave me a lift, he was very friendly, but I thought to myself there is something odd here, the way he spoke I got the idea that he was out for a good time. He told me that he was looking after his elderly mother and could only get out after she went to bed. I noticed that there was no handle on my door, and I thought that's funny, because he had leaned over and opened the door for me. I asked him about this, and he gave a lame excuse, so I thought, if he wanted to have a good time it wouldn't be with me. I put my hand into my inside pocket and pretended to have a weapon, that made him go quiet. He dropped me off near my digs, after that we got on fine and he got me home a couple of times. Sometimes the late bus, returning to the depot, picked me up, I would be the only one on board, have a good chat with the driver and a free lift as well. I quite often got lost, and once found myself walking along Heathrow perimeter wall, I never realized how big it was, it seemed never ending, eventually, I managed to flag down a taxi. Another night I was walking home, took a wrong turn and found myself walking beside a canal, there were no cars or taxis this time. Eventually I came to a police call box, they used to be all over London and looked like Doctor Who's Tardis. It was alongside a high wall, nothing for it, better than walking around all night, I went inside and picked up the receiver. I didn't have to dial a number, a policeman answered, and asked what the problem was, I explained my situation and he asked if there was a tall wall behind the box, I said yes, then he told me that I was outside Hampton Court Palace. I should turn right outside of the box; walk about two miles and I would come to a station that would take me into Hammersmith. It could only happen to me.

Another time, I was in digs with an Irishman named Paddy Maher, he was a telephone engineer, and he had a pass to get into Buckingham Palace, the Houses of Parliament and other government buildings. Sometimes he gave me a lift to work if we were going in the same direction, on one of these occasions, we discovered that his van had been stolen, this was the fourth time that had happened. He had securely locked it and it even had a steering lock attachment. The police later found it, a few streets away, still locked, they couldn't understand how it had been taken.

One Saturday, I had arranged to meet Valerie so that we could go to watch a film together, so I set off to catch the bus to pick her up. As I boarded the bus, I noticed that I was the only man on a bus full of women. They were a group of boisterous, very intoxicated, Welsh rugby fans, on their way to an international match at Twickenham. As I made my way up the aisle, they cheered each other on as they took my belt and tried to strip me. I managed to ring the bell for the bus to stop, then jumped off as it slowed down. A sobering experience and a lucky escape!

I had to phone home every so often, and as we didn't have a phone in the house, my father or mother would go to a neighbour's house, and I would call at a prearranged time. One night, I went out to phone them, but found the telephone vandalized. I went back to the digs and told Paddy, "Come on, I'll get you through", he said. We walked back to the phone box, Paddy picked up the phone, which was on the floor and proceeded to join some wires together, telling me to dial the number I wanted. When I got through, he put sixpence in and held his other hand underneath to catch it as it dropped, he continued doing that until I finished the call. When we came out of the telephone box, there were six or eight people in a line, waiting to make a call, we walked by, and as soon as we were round the corner, we ran for it.

Valerie and I decided not to stay in London as it was quite expensive, so we moved up to Lewis. We stayed with my parents for a week until I got a job and we found somewhere to stay. One day, while out for a walk, we met my old neighbour who I used to go fishing with, after the usual congratulations and hand shaking, he turned to Valerie and said, "so how was your first night"? She was dumbstruck and didn't know what to say. We all laughed when he explained that he meant on the island.

One day Valerie asked what was for dinner, I told her to see for herself as the pan was on the stove, she nearly dropped the lid on the floor, as she looked in and saw a sheep's head looking up at her. She said, "you crowd are barbaric, I want to go home to Belfast". I can't remember if she ate any of it or not.

I was working in a house in Harris one time, and met a nurse, I was telling her about Kenny, and it turned out that she was his niece. I asked how he was, as I had only seen him once since leaving London. She explained that he had been married in Edinburgh a few years back, but he had disappeared, and his bank account had not been touched. Kenny's brother was a policeman in Glasgow and had asked for Interpol to try and trace him with no luck. It was decided that he must have been murdered, a sad ending to a lovely guy.

My mother had a broody hen with chicks, and I promised Valerie, I would take her to see the chicks. When we went into the byre, the chicks were in one stall and the hen in another, when Valerie went over to pick one up, the hen flew at her, I never saw her move so fast. I had to explain to her, that the hen was just defending her brood. Sundays were very quiet, and as we were not used to that we went for a walk, and came across my mother's cockerel, which she warned us would attack if you came too near it. The next thing, I saw it on a wall, I just picked up a stone and threw it aiming to miss, the cockerel just dropped sideways, we went round to the other side of the garden wall, and found it lying on the ground, out cold, as I picked it up and put it on its feet, he just stood there for about a minute, looked at me then took off. My mother kept asking me had I seen the cockerel as she hadn't seen him for a few days, neither had I, but he eventually turned up four days later. whenever he saw me after that, he would disappear. Shortly after that, we moved out and started work in Stornoway, and were offered a caravan to rent, behind the workshop. I used to wait until the first person came to work before getting out of bed. At night when we turned the light on, as we entered the caravan, there would be a mad scurry of insects on the worktop trying to hide. I had some laughs there, one day going out on a job with the boss, we met one of the apprentices. The boss stopped him and asked where he was going, he said the other joiner had asked him to go to one of the shops, and get some tartan paint, the boss looked at me, then at the apprentice and said, "OK", as the boy left, he turned to me and said, some mothers do have them.!!! I couldn't stop myself from laughing. Apprentices were always sent next door to the blacksmiths, for a long stand, they would come back half an hour later, with a red face, after the blacksmith had kept him standing in the door all that time. I remember the first day on that job, as we were preparing to leave, I asked what tools I needed, as I did not want to carry all my tools with me. He turned to me and said, "hammer, saw and an axe", we were going over to the west side, to build a cow stall. This was a bit different from the last job I had, shop fitting in London. We had another job to do on Church St. in Stornoway, and I was told to deliver two lengths of two by one, to the other joiner that was working there. The problem was, the only transport available was an old van, which had no M.o.T. It was used as little as possible as it had hardly any brakes and had a hole in the windscreen, nothing for it but to put the timber in the van and off I went. I dropped off the timber and had a wee chat with the joiner, then the apprentice shouted the police were looking for the driver of the van parked on double lines, as I thought he was joking I took my time going to the van, sure enough two policemen were waiting for me. "Do you realize you are parked on double yellow lines"? I gave my excuses but that fell on deaf ears, as the policeman charged me. His colleague went over and said, "what happened to your windscreen"? "I'm not sure", I said, "I haven't been with them very long, but I think the passenger hit his head when the driver had to brake suddenly". As I reversed back from the kerb and drove off, I thought thank goodness they didn't check out the van, if they had I would probably have got six months. As well as the parking, I had no brakes, no hand brake, four bald tires, broken windscreen, no M.o.T. so no insurance, and you could lift the driver's seat out, was I glad to get back to the yard?

My brother and I were asked to do a job in the next village, we arranged to get the timber delivered, which was not much. We were hired to build a flat ceiling in the kitchen, we finished it in two or three nights. When we were packing up our tools, the man of the house asked if we would make some kitchen units for him, as he had the material in the shed. When we declined, he insisted that we see the timber and took us out to the shed. When he opened the shed door, we looked at each other in disbelief, the shed was full, from floor to ceiling, with kipper boxes, how he expected us to make kitchen units out of that, I don`t know. Anybody who doesn't know what a kipper box looks like, they are about 12x18 inches and made of timber as thin as 4mm and held together with staples. I remember one job we had was on a very hot day, and we were slating the roof of a house, after we had our lunch, we stretched out on the roof to take in the sun. One of the apprentices didn't like working near the gable ends and preferred the middle of the roof. When we started slating again, he looked up and decided he would sleep in the sun a bit longer, that was OK with us, we carried on slating, he eventually decided to do some work and went to get up. I think you could have heard his screams, on the other side of the island, as he tried to get up but couldn't, as we had slated round him and his clothes were under the slates, all he could see was the sky. He learned his lesson.

We went on holiday one year to a caravan park near Fort William, it was nice and quiet, we were enjoying it, when one day we found the police knocking at our door. I answered it wondering what I had done, they told me, I was to phone home immediately. We did not have a mobile phone then, so we had to find the nearest call box, which was the main office. When I phoned home, I was told that my niece Avril had died. That was a sad day for us as we left the camp site and raced up the road to catch the ferry for home.

Two of us were over in Harris working overtime till nine one night, when we headed for, home our van wouldn't start. At first, we didn't know how we were to get home, ?? we found someone to have a look at the van and got it started as the alternator had failed. We could drive it, if we kept the engine running, but we had no lights, so we borrowed a big torch from the house we were working in. We drove slowly out of Tarbert with nothing but our sidelights, as we left Tarbert the other joiner had the torch shining out the passenger window for me to see where the road was, pulling into a lay-by every time we saw a light coming towards us or behind us. We made our way like that all the way to within five miles of Stornoway, when someone passed us and spotted, we were in trouble, so he flashed on his hazard lights, and we followed him into town.

6 Northern Ireland

By this time, we had been home for about six months, with no word of a council house, though we were on the list. We decided to move, and went off to Northern Ireland, taking all our belongings with us. This consisted of four tea chests and my toolbox. We stayed with Valerie's parents for the first few weeks, a job was already lined up for me, so I started right away. It was in a factory making windows and doors and the occasional bit of furniture. We had our name down on the council list for a house, but we knew that would take a while. Finally, we got a flat to rent, it was near my work and in the centre of town. One major problem we didn't see until later, it was an upstairs flat and the bed was in a loft, only accessible by a ladder. That was OK at first, until she became pregnant with our first child, and by the time she was eight months, getting up that ladder and through the hatch was not possible. In another flat we had, that was in a village about five miles out of town, I had to take the bus into work. The first night when we went to bed, no sooner had we got in, than the bed collapsed, I don't know if it was deliberate or not, but the bed hadn't been put together properly, and we found ourselves on the floor.

The rivalry between Catholics and Protestants was immediately noticeable, and each housing estate wanted their own exclusive religious group. someone had heard that we were looking for a council house, or flat and came to see us, they said they would get us a house in the estate they were in and proceeded to tell us what to do. they would arrange for someone to break into a house, and we were to go into it, as we had found it open. This was the first time we had ever squatted, and only for one night as it turned out. I borrowed a van to get my belongings to the house. They told us how much the rent was, and I was told to call into the council offices the following morning. I should drop off the money and say that the house was empty, and I was taking up occupancy from that date, then just walk out, and that's what I did. As I walked away from the office, I heard someone shouting my name behind me, at first, I thought it was the police, but a car stopped beside me and I recognized the girl from the office I had just left, along with the housing officer. They told me that I had already been given a flat and the letter was probably in my flat. As I still had the key, I turned around and walked back Sure enough the letter was there, with the keys to a two-bedroom flat near the town centre. Then there was the long walk back to tell Valerie, we had a look at the flat and decided to take it. Back in to borrow the van again, to get the stuff I had left in the other house. I didn't know if I was coming or going, we slept on the floor that night. The following day, I took the day off, and went and bought a bed and a cooker. We had six tea chests with all our wedding presents, and everything we owned, two of them we sat on, and the other four was used as a table. For the next few weeks, as soon as I had my wages, I would buy something for the flat, a fridge, then a table and chairs, getting deeper in debt every time. The flat was on the ground floor, with three or four steps up to the front door beside a council building. The police station was directly opposite the road and there were two policemen on guard at the entrance gate, any cars coming to the flats, or the council buildings had to go to the police and get the key to the gate. I woke up one morning and realised Valerie was not in bed, she was sitting on the end of the bed puffing and panting, panic stations, she was in labour. She told me she had been sitting there since twelve thirty, and it was now four thirty in the morning. We had no phone, so I had to run to the nearest telephone box. When I got there, I found it vandalized, so I ran back to the flat to see if she was OK. I knew where another two phone boxes were, so off I went again, both boxes were vandalized, what now, I had no transport to take her to hospital, and no way of getting an ambulance. All I could think of was to speak to the police officers on guard, they told me to go up to the main door to explain, which I did, however, they were in the middle of changing shift at six am. Then I found myself explaining to about two dozen policemen that my wife was in labour. The sergeant turned to one of them, and said, "you were a male nurse take them up to maternity", an hour later our first born arrived.

We had a T.V. on hire, paying so much a week. Every couple of weeks it would break down, and I called them, they would collect it for repair. We would get it back two or three days later, this went on for months, until eventually I'd had enough. I had a bike at the time, and I cycled up to the shop, and asked to see the manager, I was told, he was in a meeting, but I could see him through a window in another room. The girls behind the counter shouted that I couldn't go in there, because they could see how angry I was, I said "try and stop me". I barged in and asked what he was playing at, I told him that I'd been paying so much for that telly, for months, and half the time it wasn't working, and if he didn't get someone down to my flat to pick it up, he could pick up the bits outside my door. "The engineer is out on a job", he said, "that's your problem", I said and walked out. I met the engineer at the door as I left. As I arrived at the flat, the engineer was coming out the door with the telly, he smiled as he walked by, we were left with a brand-new TV which never broke down.

I was always working at night doing jobs on the side, and I remember saying, cheerio to my daughter, while in Ulster and telling her I had to go out again after my tea, as I left and walked down the steps to the pavement, I heard the letter box rattling and I looked back, to see my slippers coming through the letter box after me.

As I mentioned, our flat was directly opposite the police barracks, and the army very often dropped people off there. They would jump out of the Saracen, and scatter in every direction, crouching in the drains or behind a car, anything that would give them cover. On one of those occasions, I had been watching a film on TV. and realised that I had run out of cigarettes, so I waited for the adverts to come on, then ran across the road to get some. I ran out of the door, but instead of following the footpath, I took a short cut round the corner, my mistake, as I turned the corner, there was a soldier hiding there and I nearly fell on top of him. I don't know which of us got the biggest fright, but I landed with a rifle stuck up between my legs. Another time, we were woken at 3am, by the army knocking on the door, telling us to get out, as there was a car bomb across the road. We grabbed the pram, with our daughter in it, lifted her down the steps and ran up hill in the opposite direction. A little later, it exploded, we returned home, but I was curious, so I went out to speak to a policeman and one of the soldiers. The next moment, a car was racing away from the traffic lights and shots were fired from the passenger side. I found myself in the drain, with the policeman and soldier on top of me. As quick as I could, I ran back indoors. We could see an army helicopter with a huge search light, looking for them, as they had abandoned the car further on. I heard later that they arrested two guys that night.

At the factory where I worked, there were between fifteen to twenty guys working. We had some hilarious moments, there was one labourer, his job was to sweep up the shavings and pile it up outside and set it on fire. As there was a lot of shaving and sawdust, the pile was very big, and we used Evo stick quite often, it is an adhesive that is very flammable, so, when they were empty, and the labourer wasn't looking, we sneaked out and shoved the tin into the pile of shavings, once he had set fire to the pile, he had to stand there, to keep an eye on it. when the fire caught the Evo stick container, it exploded, and shot twenty feet in the air, shavings and sawdust went everywhere. That poor labourer nearly had a heart attack, he would come in cursing and swearing calling us all kinds of names, that happened every so often. At lunch times, some would have a fight with the staple guns, they were powered by compressed air, which was used to fire staples into the timber joints. If you got hit by them in the legs or backside you would feel it. A young joiner worked with us, he was always the last to come into the tea shed, and when he came in the kettle was empty. someone shouted to put a little water in the kettle, and it would boil in plenty of time, he put some water in the electric kettle, and put it on the cooker. We told him that it was an electric kettle, so he would need to plug it in, he plugged it in and tried to set it on the cooker, but it wouldn't reach. He looked confused, I think he was brought up in the country and never saw an electric kettle.

One guy grabbed a powder extinguisher, sneaked up behind the foreman and pulled the trigger. it made a noise like a ship's foghorn, even with the clammer of all the machines, the foreman nearly jumped out of his skin, he nearly got the sack for that. I know they were wondering whether I was catholic or protestant, but I never let on. There was a one-day strike, by the protestants one week, in support of something or other, they asked me if I was going out, and I said no, as I didn't want to lose a day's wage. All that week, the Catholics were the only ones who would speak to me, I was in their good books. The following week it was the other way around, and they asked me if I was going out, and I gave them the same answer, that left them confused not knowing what I was.

We had a rush job on, and we were asked for two volunteers to come in on Easter holiday, myself and another guy volunteered. I borrowed the work truck, by the time we were finished it was dark, so I said I would take him home. He was a catholic, living on an estate on the outskirts of the town, being a protestant and going into a catholic estate was something you didn't do, but off I went onto what they called the ring road, which I knew would bring me back into the city. As I turned around a corner, I was confronted by a van on its side, and on fire. I stopped, wondering what to do, I didn't fancy going back into that estate if there was trouble, then I heard shouting, so I wound the window down. On my right, there were soldiers crouched in the ditch, and they yelled at me to "get the hell out of there". A crowd of teenagers were on the other side of the van, throwing stones at the soldiers. I could see only one way out, there was enough room to squeeze by if I put the wheels in the ditch. I slammed the van into gear, put my foot hard down, and headed for the ditch. I could see some of them jumping out of the way probably thinking who is this madman. I managed to get by and back onto the road, I don't think I was ever out in that direction again.

One time, we heard that some other companies were giving their employees a pay rise, so, we had to have the same. We raised this with the management, but as there was nothing forthcoming, we decided to go out on strike. We were standing outside when the management and the foreman came out to see what was happening. Someone had to be the spokesman, and then I heard someone shouting, Jock, I looked around to see who the idiot was and then somebody else shouted and shoved me out to the front. The manager asked me what all this was about, and I had to think quickly, I can't remember exactly what I said, but I pointed out that other companies were paying more, and we wanted the going rate. I was sure that I could get the boys back to work, if this was discussed OK, he said, and we walked back into the workshop, the shortest strike ever. The following week we had our rise. The foreman and I used to work together sometimes, and if I made a mistake, he would pick me up on it and say, you made a mistake there jock, but if he made a mistake, it would be we made a mistake there, then I would pick up on it, and say, never mind we, that was your mistake. One day he was working the tenoning machine, which had two revolving blades one above and one below a sliding platform. After switching the machine off, he saw that one blade had stopped, and went to clean the platform, without pulling it out, there was a scream of pain as he jumped back holding his hand, the top blades were still revolving, and hadn't stopped. We all rushed over to help, somebody went for bandages and towels for his mangled fingers. One guy asked, "how did you manage that"? the foreman turned to the machine, and with his other hand went to demonstrate what he had done, there was another scream of pain, he hadn't realized that the blade was still revolving. We took him to hospital to get both his hands stitched up, we couldn't help but laugh. He didn't lose any fingers, but he lost the tips of some of them, and had a few stitches, he was off work for a few weeks.

Another joiner and I were making fire doors, we had to stick a fire-retardant sheet to the back of the doors, that involved the use of Evo-stick, and needed a dust free room to do it. We took one of the benches into a corridor away from all the dust and started covering the door with the adhesive. While we waited for the adhesive to dry, we decided to have a smoke, bad idea, the door we were working on blew up, with flames about two feet high, the flames died down within seconds, and all you could see was thick black smoke. I was standing with my back to the emergency doors, so I just burst them open, the other joiner had his back to double doors leading into the workshop, the manager and everybody else came running up to see what had happened, he turned to me and said, if you want to put the place on fire, at least wait till midnight, then we can blame it on the IRA. We both got a rollicking for that. One of the joiners was getting married, and they got hold of him the week before, and stripped him completely naked. I wasn't involved in this, but I saw him afterwards, he was covered in oil, grease, eggs, sawdust, feathers, and every other thing you could think of, and shoved out the door. There was council housing on either side although a little distance away, every time he saw someone coming out of their door, he ran around the other side, he was left like that for the rest of the day. Eventually he was taken home in the back of the truck, he told me afterwards that he was in the bath for three days trying to clean himself. Two of us went to Belfast one day to do some repairs or some other job, at a site. We went in his car, which was a Volks Wagon, he asked me to drive as he didn't like driving on the motorway. That was OK if he could direct me which way to go. Driving down a street in the middle lane, as I came to traffic lights, I noticed the two cars in front of us. One turned left and the other turned right, that confused me as we were meant to go straight ahead. A man ran out to stop us and shouted there were two car bombs just ahead and across the road. We couldn't do a u turn or reverse, nothing for it. Into gear and floor it. We were about twenty yards past the first one, when it went off. It lifted the rear end of the car in the air, and we came down at nearly ninety degrees to the direction we had been going. I managed to straighten up, and we shot round the next corner doing well over the speed limit, then the next one went off. I was glad to get home that day, it still gives me the shivers when I think of how close we came to getting blown up.

One of the saws broke down one day, and an electrician was called to see what the problem was. It turned out to be a broken switch, but this had to be ordered from the manufacturers and would take about a week to arrive. However, we could still use it, if we turned the power to the machine off, open the box and push a lever down with a screwdriver. That was OK, until I went to use it one day, and forgot to turn the power off. There was a big bang and a massive flash, I found myself sitting on the floor about three feet away from the machine and seeing stars. I was helped to my feet, and checked over for burns or other injuries, I was OK but how lucky I was, that could very easy have killed me, I still don't know how it didn't. I found the ten-inch screwdriver that I used, the next day in a corner, nothing was left but the handle, and about a half inch of steel. The owner of the factory was a retired jockey and they said that was where he made his money. He was quite friendly to the work force, no airs, and graces, and didn't flaunt his wealth, except for his Rolls Royce. A couple of times he asked me to take his car home for him, as I was living less than a mile away from him. He would be going off somewhere to drink and I wasn't going to pass up the chance to drive his car. I was driving through the city like a king, thinking this is the life.

I was asked one day to deliver a load of windows to a town just outside the city, this would be fine after I finished work and had my tea. I loaded the truck and went home for my tea. I found the place and dropped off the windows. On the way back into the city, I saw an army roadblock, I had been lucky on previous occasions and had never been stopped. They used to pull every third vehicle in for a search. I started counting the number of vehicles in front of me, "oh oh it's going to be me", sure enough it was. I pulled in and was told to switch off the engine and step out. I didn't argue, I stepped out, hands on the top of the cab, spread my legs, and next thing there was a soldier on either side of me with a rifle stuck in my ribs. Another soldier began asking questions, my name, address, where was I going, where had I been? was it my vehicle? if not, who did it belong to? did I have permission to drive it? At that time, you were advised, to have written authority, to drive a vehicle that was not your own, and I didn't have that. I think without a doubt, that was my worst night ever, as I stood there with my hands on the cab, and my legs spread. If I made a move to get more comfortable, I was stabbed in the ribs, to remind me they were there. The soldier questioning me radioed his headquarters, who had to get in touch with the policeman opposite my home, they then had to find him, if he wasn't at home. When they did eventually find him, then get back in touch with army headquarters and they would then get in touch with the roadblock. I am sure I was there for at least one and a half hours. the longest in my life, my legs were still shaking when I arrived home.

One time over in Ulster, I was out on a Saturday doing a job for someone, as I was finishing off, he asked if I would like a dram. Well, it would be bad manners to say no, he poured me a large dram, and I took a big swallow, I thought my head was going to blow off, I could feel that going all the way down to my toes. I stood up spluttering, the others were laughing, then with a croaky voice, I asked them what it was, good old Irish whiskey. Poteen that was my first taste of illegal Irish whiskey.

One time I kept getting headaches, and couldn't bear to look at the light, so I made an appointment with the doctor. He took one look at me, and asked when I had broken my nose, I said I didn't know. I came out with an appointment for an x-ray at the local hospital, which confirmed that it was broken in two places. Two or three weeks later, I got an appointment to go into Newry hospital, to get it fixed. In the ward there were about six or eight of us in for various operations. The fellow beside me was about my own age, and in for the same thing, he had broken his playing rugby. I don't know who came round first, but we both got out of bed, and I said I was going to the window to see what the weather was like, came back to the bed, and lit a cigarette. At that time there was no restriction on where you smoked, well I found out that anaesthetic and smoking doesn't mix. when I woke up, the matron, and two nurses were trying to get me on my feet and into bed. I was in there for a few days, every so often I had to sit in a chair while they pulled the gauze out of my nose, it must have been a mile long. There was one hilarious moment, when a heavy built man came back from theatre, and the nurses tried to bring him round. It began with one nurse, she was lifted off her feet and into bed with him, she screamed for help. Two other nurses came running in, they landed in bed on top of him, he must have thought he was onto a good thing. with all the screaming and shouting, the matron came rushing in, shouting for them to be quiet, as this was a hospital ward. Two of the nurses had managed to get their feet on the floor and were trying to get him to loosen his grasp on the other one. The matron approached the bed shouting, "what is going on here" before she got an answer her feet had left the floor. She landed on top him, by that time the ward was in stitches laughing, and those who had stitches in were holding themselves in case they burst them, the last we saw of the matron she was running out of the ward, trying to hold her uniform together. The bed was screened off and four nurses were standing on guard in case he tried anything else. I think that was one of the best experiences I had in hospital.

 The first year I was over, I was talking to the manager, he asked me, was I going home for the summer holidays, I said no, I was hoping to hire a car for a few days and see other parts of Ireland. He offered me a loan of the company car, as it would be parked up in the yard anyway. The next day just before we knocked off, he came along and handed me the keys. Instead of a few days in a hired car, we had a fortnight, I had bought a book with all the bed and breakfasts, and hotels in every town and city. This was handy, as if we wanted to stay somewhere for the night, we just looked up the address in the book. Going through Dublin that was a nightmare, as we got lost, and found ourselves first going east, then west, and finally going back the way we come. It was like

Chinatown, when I came to traffic lights, as soon as I stopped, there was a cyclist hanging on to each mirror, and two more on the back. I finally found my way south and carried on. We drove on keeping to the east coast, and stopping, whenever we felt like it. we finally came to the southernmost point, Bantry Bay. It was the loveliest town I was ever in, there was a hill, which you could drive up and look down on the town, which we did. On the top there was an area like a picnic area, with binoculars on a stand. looking through these, you could see the whole town, and the massive oil tankers in the bay, they were that big they had scooters, to go from stem to stern. Then up the west coast, to Sligo and then we decided to cross the country and return home. I missed out on seeing Donegal and Londonderry, one of the best holidays I ever had. Then it was back to work. I was very often doing jobs on the side, and one night after my tea, I drove off to one about three miles out of the city. I finished about ten thirty or eleven o'clock and set off to go home. The guy I was doing the job for, asked which way I had come, I told him, and he told me that there was a quicker way. He gave me directions that would cut my journey time in half, turn first left, carry on past a pub, and take the next right, and I was in the city, seemed simple enough, and off I went. Half an hour later, I still hadn't come across a pub. After a wee while I came to a junction, now, decision time, which way do I go? The signs didn't mean anything to me, well I had to try some way, and took off. I noticed that the road had become narrower, and suddenly, the tar macadam stopped. I was on the border with Eire, as I could see the tar started again ten yards further on. I was completely lost, I managed to turn around, and headed back the way I came, and came to the crossroads I had passed before, then drove the opposite way. The road started narrowing again, and I found myself on the border again, drove back to the crossroads, and stopped, and started thinking what was the best thing to do. I started thinking all kinds of things, if it was used it was probably by the IRA. It was getting very late, so I drove back the way I had come originally, and came to another junction, now which way, I had no idea, completely lost and nobody to ask for directions. I sat there wondering what to do, with my petrol running low, it was completely dark no streetlights or house lights. Then I saw a light, quite a distance away, and a wee while later another light. Well at that distance, and the speed the cars were going, I realized it was the motorway. The direction the cars were going made up my mind which way to go, if I could get onto the motorway, I would either get home, or find myself in Belfast, at least I would not be lost. Fifteen minutes later, I came onto the motorway. I put my foot to the floor, and headed home, cursing myself for listening to that fellow, and his directions. I walked in the door at three thirty am to find Valerie sitting on the bed screaming at me as she was about to phone the police to report me missing. I had been driving around for four to five hours completely lost. It could only happen to me.

We had one guy started with us as a sprayer, as all the windows had to be painted when they were ready, before delivery. Well, this fellow, I can't remember his name, he was seven feet two and a half, and the second tallest man in the British Isles at the time. I was walking home from work with him one day, as he was living in the same area as me, as I was talking to him, I would look up, by the time I arrived home, I had a creak in my neck.

Woke up one morning with toothache, on the way home from work I called at the dentist, and he took me in as an emergency patient. I had a tooth pulled, and off I went home. The next morning, I still had toothache, s went to work, thinking it would eventually go away but no. I called at the dentist on my way home, he said that I had possibly had two bad teeth and pulled out another. The next morning, I still had toothache, and went to the dentist again, he took one look at me and said, "oh no, !! not you again", "oh yes", I said, "it better be the right one this time", and it was, he said it was very unusual to find three bad teeth, beside each other, at the same time.

The boss had been building a house for himself, about a mile out of the city, and sometimes called on me to do some work for him. It was built on a hill, and had four massive pillars at the front, the garage was under the main house, and as you came out of the car there was a winding stair up to the main sitting room and carried on up to the bedroom. One of the jobs was to cover the inside wall from the garage to the main room with vee lining, this was very tricky, as it was circular. The lorry driver who delivered the windows, and doors to the building sites was renovating a house about five miles out of the city and he asked me if I could give him a hand. I told him I had no way of getting out there, he told me not to worry about that as he would loan me a van. I had a look at the van when he took me out to the house one Saturday, a Morris minor, I said, "no way, the tires would not pass any test", there was no licence, the driver seat you could lift out, and you had to work the throttle with the bonnet open, with a wire coming through the window. I said if I was stopped, I would be jailed, he persuaded me to take it, and off I went. As I said earlier, staying opposite the police station I had to stop beside the police, and turn the wheels to the kerb, as there was no hand brake, step out and ask for the key to the gate, drive the van in, and give the key back. Eventually, I managed to get the wire for the throttle in through a hole under the dash, which helped a little? I had that van for five or six weeks, and I was never stopped by the police or army. I don't know if I was ever insured for any of the vehicles I drove. It was only in later years I thought of that. One time doing a homer, in a big posh house, there was an Irishman working as a gardener with his three sons. as I was finishing up and collecting my tools, the lady of the house came and asked if I would like a dram, well I was not the type to say no, so I said, yes thank you. "I wonder if Paddy and the boys will take a dram", she said, as she walked over to the door leading onto the garden, she took a few steps into the garden and shouted, "Would you like a dram"? "Thank you, ma am, that would be very nice", a few minutes later she came out with five whiskeys on a tray, handed one to me, and then went out to the gardener with the tray. Paddy took the tray and thanked her, then went and sat down on a bench. As the lady of the house went inside, I went and sat down with the gardener for a chat, I said to him "are you calling your boys over for their dram"? "No, they don't drink", he sat there and downed the four drams himself.!!!

I bought a bike to cycle to work, it was a lady's bike with a basket on the front, which was handy, for my flask and sandwiches, or so I thought. I jumped on and peddled past the police gates where two policemen were on guard, then the speed bumps. As I came onto them the flask had a mind of its own and jumped out. I lost four or five going over that speed bump. The police used to shout to me, is that another new one. Believe it or not, I used to go to church every Sunday, even when I was in London, we were thinking of getting our daughter baptized. One day I looked out the window and saw the minister walking down the road, so I ran out and asked him. He looked in his diary and said, "no problem", he gave me a date, and told me to go to the manse where his daughter would explain everything. A big difference from getting the other two done after I came home, I had to go in front of the elders and answer questions on the catechism.

Every Saturday, a woman came down the road, she had five or six kids varying in age from ten to about four, I used to call them the ducks, they would hold on to each other's jackets, starting with the eldest hanging on to his mother, then the next in height, till it came to the youngest who was practically running to keep up.

We were told one night that an incendiary device had been left in some shops in the town centre. We waited inside until they exploded just in case we were caught up in any trouble. Then the fires started, four shops went up in flames. They were about two thousand yards away from us, but we could see it from the window. One of the shops was a hardware shop, they sold gas containers, well, as you can imagine, there was a massive bang, and the gas containers shot up into the air for about twenty yards. It was like Guy Fawkes again.

They were going out on strike for this that and the other, and one time, everybody had been out on strike for nearly a week, and rations were running low. One of my workmates suggested going across the border, as he had young kids to feed. Off we went to the nearest town across the border, through the check point, and into the nearest town, we got our supplies, and headed for home. As we approached the border post we were flagged down, and I thought, crikey!! What's the family going to think, caught smuggling on the Irish border. The guards put their heads in the window, and said, "right what have we here"? we didn't try to conceal anything, we had about a dozen loaves, twenty pints of milk, and about six dozen eggs. "Having a party are you"? When we explained they just said, "that's OK, have a good day" and let us go, my first experience of smuggling. One time, a friend from work, suggested going out on a pub crawl. He knew all the pubs, and if they were protestant pubs or catholic, he would tell me before going in. He suggested if we were asked who we were, in a protestant pub, I was jock and he was Jim, if it was a catholic pub, I was Paddy, and he was jimmy. He knew a lot of people and would say to me as we had a drink, that fellow over there, is in the IRA and had been jailed for something or other, that fellow in the corner had lost half his side when a bomb he was working on went off, and the two at the bar they were known to be in the UDA. We had a very good night without any mishaps, until these two guys came in and sat opposite us, two Japanese guys. One of them started on about his new watch, he could use it as a phone, the other not to be outdone, said his phone was in his ears and he didn't have to do anything when it rang, just press a button, and speak. Jimmy said he was going to the toilet, when he came back a few minutes later one of the Japanese guys started pointing behind him, there was about two feet of toilet paper coming out of his trousers. Jimmy says, "it's all right I am just getting a fax through"!!! there was no more talk about fancy phones. Jimmy told me later when he went home his wife opened the door in her nighty, at the time I thought that it was a funny place for a door!!

We decided that Northern Ireland had become very dangerous, and by then we had another addition to the family. we planned to move back to Lewis, which was not going to be easy, as a removal firm would charge us about eight hundred pounds, money we did not have and couldn't afford. I decided to look around for a suitable sized van, to take all our belongings and drive myself. I put the word out for what I was looking for, and then I heard of one that might be suitable. It was in a scrap yard in Belfast, so I went to see it, it was sitting in a corner there, so I had a look at it. It was about the right size, but there were a few problems, it didn't have a battery, it had hardly any brakes, no hand brake at all, and I was told it sometimes jumped out of top gear, you had to keep it in gear with your hand. It had a good six-cylinder engine, which started with the first turn, so I bought it for eighty pounds. The next morning, I took it to a local garage to get the brakes and the hand brake fixed, I was told that to fix it, it would cost more than the van was worth, but they did their best, it might last till I got home to Lewis and that was all I needed. I arranged for Valerie to go by plane with the kids. and I started packing the van, as I got nearer the back doors, I realized I had nowhere to sleep, so I left enough room between the furniture and the roof, and shoved a mattress in there, to sleep on. I was booked on the Larne to Stranraer ferry in the evening, and as I pulled up at the check point at Larne, there was a policeman on one side, and a soldier on the other. As I came to a stop with grinding brakes, I pulled the handbrake, and it came away in my hand. As I laid the handbrake on the seat beside me, I looked at the policeman then at the soldier. The policeman looked at the soldier and then at me, and just asked where I was going, the usual questions, they looked at each other and told me to carry on. I can just imagine their conversation, as I drove on to the ferry. Driving off at the other side I carried on up towards Ayr, but thought I should bed down for the night, as it was getting dark. I pulled into a lay-by, getting into bed was another thing, as I had to climb all the furniture to get onto the mattress. When I got on the mattress it was so close to the roof, I was not able to turn. The following morning, I carried on up the A77 and into Glasgow. I had arranged to call in and see my aunt on the way, I knew where they lived but finding my way there, was another thing. I found myself in the city centre, and that was a nightmare, driving a three-ton truck through the city, with no brakes, and trying to hold it in gear with my left hand, while looking for signposts or directions that would help me. I thought to myself what in heavens name have I done to deserve this. Eventually, I saw the sign for the Clyde tunnel and headed for that, as I came out the other side, it was completely different from the way I remembered, they were busy with new road works. I could see my aunt's house on Maryhill but couldn't get to it. The road was leading me away in the other direction. I eventually managed to turn back and found their house. After a cup of tea and a chat I headed off, my uncle directed me on to the A82 and off I went again, I remember coming down Kinloch Leven, and it jumped out of gear on me, I think my hand was getting tired, and with no brakes I thought this is it. I began to gain on some holiday caravans, as the nearest caravan's number plate disappeared from in front of me, they started going uphill. They were pulling away from me, that was a close one. The rest of the journey was uneventful, I can't remember anything happening. I travelled on the Harris ferry, and driving up the Ardhasaig hill at eleven pm, a car pulling a caravan decided to stop in the middle of the hill. The driver stepped out and started flashing a torch, as if he was looking for a place to park. He soon jumped back in as I was right behind him, revving the engine and blowing my horn, while trying to hold it in gear. I didn't like the idea of coming this far, then wrecking it when I was only ten miles from home. I arrived at the house about midnight.

7 Homeward Bound

First thing in the morning, I was off to town to look for a job, as I was nearly broke, first person I recognized was my old boss, who took me on, and told me to start the following Monday, that was great, at least I had work, and would be bringing money in. Shortly after we managed to let a house nearby that was lying empty, then the next child arrived, and we were given a council house in Balallan, and that was me, back to thumbing a lift back and fore to work, until I saved up to buy a car. We were working on a house in Harris, it was owned by an international banker and had their main residency in Paris and another house in the USA, this was their holiday home. One of the jobs we had to do, was to fit a winding stair, from the lounge to the bedroom, they came up for a week while we were working there, and on this occasion the wife decided to come up the ladder and see what it looked like, she stepped on to the joist and the next thing she slipped and went through the ceiling. the joiner nearest her made a grab for her, to stop her going any further, what he grabbed was her breasts, but held her from going any further, as we ran up to get a hold of her hands, and pulled her up, as we got her on her feet, we asked was she alright and was she hurt.? I am OK, she said, thanks just my pride, I should not have been so nosy, as she went down the ladder, she turned to the first joiner and said, at least you had a good handful, we couldn't stop laughing. We were told to be careful with the furniture and fittings as they were very expensive. On one occasion we arrived to find the living room flooded, and a 12 feet by 12 feet hand crafted Chinese rug that had cost over £10000, floating in 2 inches of water. We turned off the water, and phoned the office, then arranged for a plumber to come over. As we moved the furniture, which luckily was not damaged, we wondered how to dry the rug. Six of us went over the following day, and it took us most of the day to take it outside in two wheelbarrows. We left it hanging over a wall and fence for at least a month to dry out, luckily it was Springtime and we had little rain and a good breeze. When we finally got it back in the house, it was a lot lighter than when it went out. I don`t know if it shrank or not.

While I was working one day, my boss asked me to go with him to look at a job in Harris. This turned out to be Ardvourlie Castle, he told me it was a renovation job. It had been bought by an English man, who wanted to do it up for bed and breakfast. When we walked in, we had to chase the sheep out, and from the ground floor you could see the sky. We were working on that job for the next two years off and on. The apprentice joiners were always annoying the brickies, so the two brickies and the labourer decided to sort them out. They had a forty-five-gallon drum full of water, which we used for mixing cement, they got a hold of the two of them, and one after the other, the labourer, who was a big strong fellow lifted them into this drum headfirst until their head hit the bottom, then pulled them up, that stopped any more larking about. We used to play tricks on them as well, like nailing or screwing their toolboxes to the floor, or filling their lunchbox with sawdust and shavings, after they had their last tea break. We had one labourer, Callum and he was always up to mischief, while we were at our tea break one day the conversation turned to vegetables, and one of the joiners, Norman asked where he could get a bag of turnips. Callum said," I can get you a bag of turnips no problem, I know the farmer very well". "Can you, how much "? "I think they are £3 a bag". "Get me two", he said. "OK I'll bring them in tomorrow". Callum came in the following morning and showed Norman a turnip, and the two bags. "That's great, put them in the boot of my car", and proceeded to pay him. When Norman went home that night he put the bags in the shed, and told his wife, "good", she said "I'll get one for our tea" , as she opened the bag she couldn't use any of them, because they been half eaten either by worms or the cattle, Callum had lifted the turnips from the field, that the farmer had thrown out to the sheep and cows. He spent the next week trying to avoid him.

Norman was obsessed by the amount of money being paid to men working on the Channel tunnel. He began asking if anyone knew the phone number of companies, because he wanted to go down there. None of us could help, so he tried the job centre. Finally, Callum said he knew someone he could get the number from. The following morning Callum handed Norman a slip of paper with a telephone number on it, "that's great I'll ring them tonight". When Norman had his tea that night he sat down and rang the number he was given, it was answered by a woman, who said, "Hi this is Sexy Sue". Norman put the receiver down thinking he had dialled the wrong number. A wee while later he tried again making sure it was the right number. "Hi this is sexy Sue", then it dawned on him, Callum had picked up a number for a chat line from the back page of the Sun. There was no more mention of the Channel tunnel. Callum had to avoid him for the next fortnight.

 One time we were on holiday, staying at a camp down on the west coast. I can't remember the name of the place. It was directly opposite Liverpool, and just an hour's drive away. Valerie had an aunt and cousins there, so we decided to take the day and visit them. We found their house, and spent the day with them, and on the way back decided to go into Liverpool, to do some shopping. After about an hour we decided it was time to go back to the camp, we had left the car in a disused car park, and just walked up to the shops. Well could we find that car park again, we were going round in circles for nearly an hour. I suggested asking a policeman, when one of the girls remembered passing a certain shop, so we carried on down past it, and walked round the corner, and there it was all on its own, that was a relief. That goes to show what my sense of direction is like. Coming back to the camp I was one day sunning myself in front of the caravan, when a car stopped, and the window came down. A chap I didn't know shouted to me in Gaelic, we had a good time from then on, as our kids and theirs played together while we had a few drinks at the bar.

When we were in Balallan the children had a schoolteacher, a nice lady but the kids were afraid of her. She had a squint in one eye, so the children all thought she was looking at them. She went into town one day, and as she was turning around the corner at Church Street, someone bumped into her. "Look where you are going", she said, quick as a flash the other guy responded, "You go where you are looking".

I remember our daughter coming home on holiday, she had a friend with her. They went out on Friday night as usual, and while walking down the street, heard the breaking of glass and within minutes came across the chemist shop with the window broken. A little later, they were sitting in the car park when a guy came over to them and offered them some cosmetics which they declined. The police had been called and as they had been seen in the vicinity they were reported to the police. I can't remember if they were questioned while they were in the car park or not. About six in the morning, I was woken up by a loud knocking on the door, when I opened the door, I was met by a policeman and a sergeant, they wanted to know where the girls were. At that time, I didn't know any of this, but they insisted that they speak to the girls. Although I explained that they had only returned a short while before and they were asleep, I had to wake them up and the young policeman started examining their hands. This really annoyed me as I knew my daughter wouldn't be involved in anything like that and told them so. I asked the sergeant to let them sleep, then as soon as they had their breakfast, I would personally take them to the station The sergeant put his hand on his mate's shoulder and nodded for them to go. After they had breakfast and been questioned by me, I took them down to the police station. As we arrived, my daughter shouted and pointed at a man coming out of the station and said that was the man who offered them the cosmetics. They gave a statement to the police and the man was arrested. They were later called as a witnesses, but this was cancelled as he had pled guilty.

 We had some hilarity at work as well, we were sent to renovate an old house in one of the villages. Before leaving, in the morning, one of the joiners asked the boss, if he wanted us to keep the copper pipes, and plumbing work from the kitchen, he said, OK, it might come in handy. When we arrived, he proceeded to open all the joints, and threw them out of the window. After lunch he decided to go out and tidy up, he couldn't find anything, but he could hear a squeaking noise round the end of the house. When he went to see what it was, he found another joiner had filled about four bags full of copper tubes, ready to be sold for scrap. you could hear the curses and name calling, as he chased him down the road. The other joiner was always looking for scrap that he could sell to give him extra money for a pint.

One year we decided to go back to Northern Ireland for a holiday. I worked out the ferry times and how long it would take me, then we left the house about 5 in the morning to catch the ferry in Tarbert, and drove on through Skye, and onto the mainland. It wasn't long after leaving the ferry when my wipers stopped working, as I knew nothing about engines, we decided to stop at a garage in Fort William to get it checked. I needed a new wiper motor. I hadn't accounted for breakdown costs, so told them I would leave it for now, and headed off for Stranraer. As we drove into the ferry terminal, the car park was empty, but I saw someone at the far end, and drove over to him. He asked if I was for the ferry, and I said "yes", "OK drive straight on". I don't think he even checked my ticket, we arrived at our destination about midnight. The following day I went to get my wiper motor fixed at a small garage nearby, as he was asking me where I came from, he took out a fuse and fitted a new one, that was it wipers working. I would have been out of pocket by well over a hundred pounds and would have missed the ferry if I had listened to the first garage. Driving into Belfast on the motor way, we could see the Harland and Wolff crane in the distance, holding up a red double Decker bus, you could see it from five or six miles out. On the way back, I remember it was a Sunday and the motorway was quiet, hardly a car on it. The kids were sitting in the back, and they started saying there was a car coming up behind us. As I looked in the mirror, I thought at that distance it can't be a car, it must be a big van or lorry. I was travelling at about seventy, looking in the mirror I could not make out if it was a van or lorry. I soon found out, as within minutes, a double Decker bus came flying past, with just a mechanic driving it, he must have been travelling well over a hundred miles an hour, as he left us standing. I was telling someone about it afterwards and was told that if one of the local buses broke down, they would have to get one from the depot in Belfast. Boarding the ferry in Larne, it was quite full, but I managed to get a seat for Valerie and the kids, and I got a seat out in the corridor, every now and then I would go and check on them, then come back to the same seat. On one of these occasions, I noticed that we were coming into berth, and as I went to sit down in my usual seat, I turned to the fellow beside me who looked like a farmer who had never been on a boat. I turned to him and said, we are just coming into berth, he had not moved from that seat in all the times I was there. With a startled look he half jumped out of his seat, and with a broad Irish accent said, "be jeezus, I never realized we had left". I don't know what he thought we had been doing for the past two hours, we had an uneventful drive home.

I was always keen on work, and knew that if you didn't work, you didn't get paid. So, imagine my thoughts when I woke up one morning, and went out to go to work. It had been snowing and all I could see of the car was the roof, nothing for it but to dig myself out. It took about an hour to dig a track out to the main road. I had no sooner made it to the main road, than the snowplough came along, and I followed him into town arriving at work at midday, just in time for lunch. On another occasion a blizzard started, and we decided to go home early, by the time we got on the road there were drifts everywhere, with cars off the road, and stuck in drifts. A journey that normally took a half hour, took me three and a half hours to get home. To make extra money I volunteered for call outs, which meant, sometimes being called by the police at all hours of the night, when someone had broken a shop window in town. On one of these call outs, on New Year's Day, and believe it or not I only had one drink, and that was at midnight, I had to go up to the castle, and board up some windows that had been broken. As I parked on the pavement beside the castle, I had a word or two with the police. when finished I jumped into the truck, looked behind me, saw the road leading into the castle, and started reversing back, not realizing there was a three-foot drop beside it. Next thing, I felt the back end of the truck dropping, and a loud crunch. I stepped out to see the damage, the back end was resting on the axle, and the rear wheels were two feet off the ground. I was going nowhere. I had to walk back and tell the boss what had happened, we had to get a crane to lift it on to a lorry, to take it back to the yard. It could only happen to me.

One of the fellows in the village was building a house and asked me to give him a hand, that was OK it was extra money for me. I was working away one Saturday when I heard this noise and I looked behind me to see a goat eating the nails I had been using. I chased it outside and no sooner had I put him out than he would be in again. As there was no door on the building, I decided to put up a barricade and nailed a sheet of plywood across the bottom half of the door, which left it 6ft from the ground to the top of the ply, that should keep him out. While I carried on working, there were a few head butts and then everything went quiet. I walked down the hall to see where he had gone, only to see him balanced on his stomach on top of the sheet of ply and then finally toppling into the hall and on to his feet and off down where the nails were. In the end I had to put up a barricade on the outside to stop him getting near the door.

We were working on a renovation one time; I think it was the same one I mentioned earlier. It was coming up to Xmas and it was snowing outside. The day we were going on holiday, the fireplace had been taken out, and it was left with a big open area where the fire had been.

Someone started a fire in the opening, to get rid of the rubbish, and keep ourselves warm. The next thing we heard was a roaring sound, the chimney was on fire. If we had let it carry on the roof would probably soon be on fire. There was no water available, as it had been turned off, panic stations, nothing for it but buckets of snow, and someone with a length of two by one down from the top, to scrape the burning soot down the chimney. A couple of guys inside were sweeping up the burning soot, and taking it outside, we made it.

We were allocated a new council house in Balallan, and lived opposite a family with five kids, who were always in trouble. I came out the door one Sunday to find them throwing mud pats at our gable wall. I lost my temper and marched over to their door and thumped on it. Both parents came out, and I pointed out what their children had done, and demanded they get it cleaned, or they were in trouble. For the next four hours, they used buckets of water and hoses, trying to clean it off, even standing on each other's shoulder to reach some. I didn't let them off, until I was satisfied with the result, they kept well away from us after that.

 We were trying to get a house in town to be near work, and finally we got one. When we moved our furniture in, getting used to living in town again and settling in. I had a problem, how do I get all the peats for the fire, which we had left at the previous house, over to town? I borrowed the works lorry at the weekend, I had been going back and forth the previous week, filling bags of peat, so I had quite a load on the lorry. On the outskirts of town, going down towards the roundabout, I touched the brake to slow down slightly but nothing happened. No brakes, to say I panicked is an understatement, I was doing thirty-five miles an hour with a load of peats in the back pushing me faster. I managed to get into a lower gear, which slowed it down slightly, but not enough. I made the decision, that as I was going too fast to turn into town towards the house, I would go straight on, as the road levelled off. Then, if a car was coming on to the roundabout, at the same time, I would pull on the hand brake, which they call the dead man, and hope for the best. If I had, the load would be all over the road. Looking left and right as I came onto the roundabout, with relief, no cars, as I shot across, and managed to get it into a lower gear, from then on, it was first gear all the way to the house.

I remember one Christmas eve waiting for the kids to go to sleep. Robert had one bedroom and the girls another, as we walked into Roberts's bedroom to leave Santa`s present on his bed, I noticed a mouse, sitting quite the thing on the pillow beside his head. As I dropped the presents and jumped to catch it, Valerie screamed which woke the girls up, but not Robert. The girls woke up and came in to see what was happening, then ran back into their own bedroom when they realized it was a mouse. As I chased it round the room it got out and went into the girl's room, which made them jump onto their beds, more screams and shouting to let me know where it was. It eventually managed to escape and went down a hole in the floorboards. The following morning, I caught it in a trap under the kitchen sink. All this time, with all the screams and shouting Robert never woke up, that is one Christmas eve I shall always remember. We were in that house a couple of months, and realized we couldn't open the windows, as they were rotten, I kept complaining, but nothing was happening. When going to bed one night I was feeling a draft, and asked Valerie if she had opened a window, walking over to see, I noticed the curtains moving. When I pulled back the curtains, the windowsill was so rotten that the glass had dropped through and was resting on the concrete sill. The following day was a Sunday, so I wrote a letter to the head of the council and a copy to their legal department. At that time if I was working nearby, I would call in for my ten o'clock tea break. Tuesday, I called in, and who was there, but the council clerk of works and a joiner, they were measuring up for new windows. He said that it was a similar style of house to another scheme they were working on, they would take the windows they were going to use there and do this one first. I can't remember what I put in that letter, but it soon got the result we wanted.

I mentioned earlier about being in hospital at various times in my life. On one occasion just after New Year. I had a bad cold and started coughing up blood and was persuaded to go and see the doctor. when I told him he just wrote a letter and sent me over to the county hospital for an x-ray. I kept working as normal, I still had to earn a living. About teatime the following morning Valerie phoned my work and asked to speak to me, she said that the doctor had been at the house looking for me. She was to get hold of me immediately and get me out to hospital in Inverness. As she was not the type to play jokes like that, as soon as I had my tea, I booked my flight to Inverness. When I arrived home that night, I phoned the doctor and was told that whoever took the x-ray was looking at them as he was going across on the ferry, and when he saw mine, he knew I had TB and phoned the doctor from the pier. I was on two large tablets a day for two or three weeks. I had a brother who died before I was born, if it was TB I don't know, but I must have had it when I was younger, and the scar must have opened up again. I was back to work after a month.

8 Moving On

On one occasion I remember a funny incident, it happened I think, when we were on that holiday I mentioned earlier. I was asked to go and see a relative in hospital in Glasgow, although I was going to bypass Glasgow I agreed. I decided as I didn't know Glasgow very well, I would park the car somewhere, then get a taxi to the hospital. I found a multi-story car park, left the car, and went down to the street, there was a taxi rank there, so we jumped in I told the driver where we wanted to go. "No problem" he said, as he drove off, "there it is", and he pointed up the hill to our right, with all the one-way system and traffic lights, it took us about five minutes to get to the hospital, and less than a minute to walk down the steps to the street again, he only charged a pound, and he never stopped talking.

We decided to have a proper holiday one year, I can't remember if were invited over to Canada, or did we just say we were going, any way we saved up and off we went. It was a seven-hour flight, and very smooth. We stayed with Valerie's sister, just outside Toronto, and had a good time there, seeing the sights and shopping. We were in Toronto one time, and one of the girls wanted to go to the toilet, my brother-in-law took her into a hotel, and we waited for her to come out. When she did, she was bright red, and we asked what was wrong, she said, I think someone was watching me, how do you think that we asked? Well, when I stood up from the toilet, I was tidying myself up when the toilet flushed, and I was not near it, we could not stop laughing. We were in a multi-story clothes shop, I think it was three floors, when we realized there was no sign of the youngest. I was up and down the stairs looking for him, Valerie and her sister going into a panic, they decided to go down to security at the front door and report him missing. Off they went while I carried on looking. There were the usual questions, "what did he look like", "small and blonde", "What was he wearing"? "Trainers and jeans" "How old was he"? You can imagine the security guy's face when they said twenty-one. We eventually found him, but I still laugh when I remember that. We went to the CN tower, that was brilliant, a lot bigger than the Post Office Tower in London, the lift in the P O. tower came down so fast, and stopped so suddenly, that you thought you had left your stomach at the top. The C.N tower was as smooth and fast; you didn't feel a thing. There was a glass floor, and see everything below, the cars were like dots, and you could see for miles around. When you went outside you were nearly blown off your feet, you could feel the building swaying. I went shopping with my brother-in-law one day, and went into a shopping mall, it was massive, I think the car park was about the size of Stornoway. When we came out, it was getting a bit dark, and I said, "how do we find the car in this lot", "no bother", as he pressed his ignition key, the boot of the car opened, and started going up and down, as if to say, I'm over here, modern technology. Sitting on the veranda with a drink, and taking in the sun, I looked across the street, something was puzzling me, I thought to myself, the people in one of the houses seemed to be very big, and then a door opened in the room I was looking at, I realized that it was a T.V. Screen that was projected on to the wall. Then it was time to go home. If the flight over was calm, this one was the opposite, we were an hour out of Toronto, and the stewardess was pouring out a cup of tea for me, when the captain came on to tell us to tighten our belts, as we had to go through a storm. There was a plane below us and another one above, so the only thing he could do was go straight through. I was in the middle of having my tea and had just time to swallow it when we started rolling. We arrived safely at Glasgow, and then home.

I was driving to a job one day with the work truck, and as I came to a junction, I noticed a cyclist had stopped on my right. I had the right of way, but as I passed him there was an almighty bang, and my truck was thrown into the oncoming traffic. As I desperately tried to avoid a head on collision with another driver, I just hit its mirror. Looking back to see what had happened I noticed a bike in the middle of the road, and a man leaning over someone. As I ran back, I was thinking I couldn't have hit that cyclist. Then I noticed a car headfirst into a wall, the car hadn't stopped at the junction. The driver hadn't been wearing a seat belt, so when he hit the side of my truck he went through the windscreen and landed on the road. I was breath tested and passed; the other driver was taken to hospital.

We were sitting in the house on a Sunday night, when Valerie asked for money for the rent, which was due the following morning. I gave her the money, and I gathered all the rent books from previous years, and started to add up the money we had given the council in previous years, the total amount was enough to buy two houses. I vowed then, that if we got a proper house, I would buy it. Shortly afterwards we got the house we are in now and bought it. As soon as we moved in, I decided to make the kitchen bigger, so I dismantled a wall separating the kitchen and cellar and made it one big kitchen. I had to plaster the wall and ceiling where the other wall had been. Being in the trade I knew someone who would give me a bit of plaster and save me buying a big bag. I set up a scaffold for myself and mixed the plaster on a board on the table. After mixing, I had to wet the wall so that it would bond better. I turned round to get the plaster and found my trowel stuck in the plaster; it had all gone solid. He had given me some old plaster which had been half used, I had to get a hammer and chisel to get my trowel out. I don't know if he did it deliberately or not, but he gave me more the following day. The next day halfway through plastering the wall, my scaffold collapsed and part of it hit me in the ribs, and that was me with a cracked rib for the next couple of months. It seems that cancer is doing its best to blight my life, as my wife is fighting it for the third time. I had been in hospital several times throughout my life, for various things, one of them was gall stones, I was admitted a couple of times, and then they decided to remove them. I went in on a Sunday, operation on Monday and out on Tuesday and I walked down for the paper in the afternoon, after having keyhole surgery. Years ago, you couldn't do anything for six weeks, and you would be off work for eight.

I was going to bed one night; it was bitter cold and freezing. My youngest, who at the time was working till midnight in a hotel, when he came home, he went to put his bike in the shed, but couldn't, and realized someone was asleep on the floor. He came running in to tell me, and I ran out and found that a tramp had found the door unlocked, and decided to bed down for the night, I don't know who got the biggest shock, my son, or the tramp. It reminded me of a joke Billy Connolly told about the wife who was buried in the garden, with her backside sticking up, when asked why she was like that, he said that it was a good way of parking his bike. The poor tramp was shaken with the cold and refused to come into the house. We made tea and toast for him, and I think the first cup went down in one. He didn't have a word of English, but we gathered he was German, and had come across three days previously. We knew that if we left him there, we would have found him dead in the morning. As he wouldn't come into the house, there was nothing else for it, we called the police, when they arrived, he became agitated, and said repeatedly, "I got papers", until we finally calmed him down and he left with the police. We found out later that he was put up in a hotel, at least he had one warm night.

I used to work a lot at nights, and very often through the holidays, on one occasion during the summer holidays, I was working at one of my regular clients, when Valerie phoned me at about nine O clock. I thought something had happened and asked what was wrong, she said, "your boss phoned the house asking if you were OK", "why"? I said, because your holiday finished yesterday, you are supposed to be at work today. Oh crikey!! I Packed up my tools and shot off, he knew where I had been and just laughed.

My cousin and two others were in the pub on a Friday, and we were going to a dance. He had just bought a brand-new Austin a35, as we walked over to the pier where the van was parked. We met two policemen doing their rounds, "are you going home then boys"? We are off to the dance." good, take it easy on the way over, and take care". "Thanks, goodnight" and that was us with a carryout each under our arm off we went. The dance was about twelve miles from town, now if you have a carry out, you don't leave it in the boot, by the time we were about a mile away from our destination, we were well away, including the driver. I remember vividly driving up a hill doing about twenty miles an hour, and suddenly the van was on its side. As I landed on top of the driver, I had the problem of opening the door which I had to push upwards and pulling the rest out. As we found out later the only damage to the new van was a wee scratch on the Sill. How do we get out of this. We had a dance to go to, the four of us went round the back, lifted the back on to the road then, round the front, and lifted the front onto the road. OK jump in and off we went. We found out later, as we drove through the village, we were seen driving up the road doing about twenty, by someone sitting by the fire. He got up and said to his wife he was going out to give us a hand. He put his shoes on, grabbed his jacket from behind the door, and went out the door. As he looked down the road there was no sign of us, he turned to his wife, and said he must be seeing things and walked back in, confused.

I had one hilarious incident while out on one of my homers. I had to demolish a wall between the kitchen and sitting room to make a bigger sitting room and convert the garage into a kitchen. I was to do the joinery and John; the owner was doing the plumbing and the electrical work. When I took the partition down all the switches and sockets were lying all over the place, so john decided to put them under the floor until he got time to disconnect them properly, as he was working through the day as well. That was OK for a day or two until one night when we went in, they had a big black Labrador, and guess what, the

Labrador went over to where the holes in the floor were and lifted his leg, well, there was an almighty bang and a flash, and that poor dog yelped, did a somersault two feet in the air, came down did two half circles on the floor, and ran out the door howling. He had peed right onto one of the switches, and nearly put the house on fire. We didn't see the dog again until the following day, he must have been licking his wounds all night. When we finally stopped laughing, we decided to get rid of the cables in case anything else happened.

I had a call at work one day, to say that my son, who was fourteen at the time, had been attacked while coming home from school. I went home and found him in a state and asked him what had happened. He told me that a fellow I knew, who lived not far away, had grabbed him by the neck, and accused him of breaking into his garage and stealing some tools. I knew my son, and knew that he wouldn't have done that, so after I had my tea, I waited in the car outside his house until he came home, which was not very long. I called him over, and asked what was going on, and he told me that my son had been seen and he must have taken the tools. I told him he was wrong, and I could prove it, but first he would have to come up to the house and apologize, if not I was getting the police, as he knew as a thirty-five- or forty-year-old, had just assaulted a fourteen-year-old in front of plenty of witnesses, and I drove off home. He came to the door a few minutes later but still insisted that my son was a thief. I told him he would either apologize, or I would phone the police, when he wouldn't, I grabbed the phone and dialled the first two numbers, he then stopped me, and gave a weak apology, and asked me how I could prove that it was not him. I asked him what date this had happened, and he told me. I knew my son had kept his flight ticket stubs so I told him to bring them in, we were away on holiday a day before they went, and came back the day after them, he left the house very sheepish. We found out later it was his own sons, who had accused him, they were never out of trouble. The three kids were not seen on the street for about a month after that, and every time since then they crossed the street to avoid us.

I have always been proud of my family, and what they have achieved in life, but that was severely shattered over twenty-five years ago, when my eldest, who had gone through university, and took a year off to visit Australia, came home, and announced that she was severing all contact with us, and left for the mainland. Well, to say it hit us hard, is an understatement, we don't know why, and she never told us. It affected the whole family; we were back and fore from the doctor and sometimes the hospital, on antidepressants and sleeping pills. We were lucky that the youngest was in college in Glasgow and didn't see how it had affected the rest of the family. I know that it did affect him, as the two of them were very close, and he doted on her, that made matters worse. I am sure, to this day, he still can't get over what she did. Talking to a psychiatrist at the hospital didn't help, and being on anti-depressants, sleeping pills and drinking, which is a lethal combination. I was going to work like a zombie. I remember I had eleven hours sleep in as many days, crawling up stairs to bed and lying there thinking, what had I done? Was it my fault? and what could I do? I never got an answer. I know that it did impact on my work, and my boss at one time asked me to take a few weeks off, as he knew the situation, but I refused, and said that if I stopped work, I would probably never work again. I am glad to say he understood and kept me on. I needed something to take my mind off it, if only occasionally. Sitting thinking at two and three in the morning, and drinking, I had some dark thoughts that I don't like to mention. Yes, I was suicidal. I think the turning point came, when I woke up in hospital, with a cut on my head, and was discharged in the morning and sent home by taxi with a note, for me to be kept an eye on, as I had a head injury. Arriving home in the taxi, I met my son going into the same taxi, to take him to the airport, and back to college. Sitting down that night I decided that whatever dark thoughts I had, was not going to help me, or my family. back to the doctor the following week, discussed the situation with her, and asked to be taken off the tablets, she was not pleased at that request, but agreed to reduce the dose. I was eventually off the sleeping pills, and a few months later the anti-depressants, I was still taking a drink or two, but at least I was in control of my life. All this took place over a few years, although Valerie is still on anti-depressants. We found out later that she was married in Glasgow, with four of a family, we did not try to get in touch, as doing so would probably open old wounds. writing the last two pages took four times the time it took to write the first page, as it is an episode, I would like to forget but will always be etched on my mind. My son, who was working in Glasgow at the time, met a lovely lady, not only in appearance but in personality, he made the right decision and got married. The result of that were two lovely grand kids. After a couple of years in rented accommodation they decided to buy a house, and they got one, just round the corner from where they were, then I got the call to arms could I go down and fit a kitchen for them, and a few other things which I was glad to do. His sister who was working in Inverness at the time, was still single and had a good job, she was trying to buy a house, but was gazumped a couple of times, which annoyed her. She went to visit her brother in Glasgow one weekend and found the price of houses a lot lower there. Nothing for it, she was going to move there if she got a house. The first one she saw with a suitable price, she told her sister-in-law to check it out, and was warned to leave it, a second one came up, and again asked to look it over, and was told to go for it. She put an offer in for it, and got it, that was it, worked her notice, and gave me a call to help her move, which I did, and helped with whatever alteration she wanted done. I was glad to help and see her settling down. She had been living in a flat three floors up. It was bad enough climbing three floors, but carrying things down was different, even the removal man, was surprised how much stuff she had gathered in a few years. She had asked for a price for the removal but had to get another van. She is now settled in her own home, with a good job, and living close to her brother, and can see her nephew and niece. I don't know if I would have the guts, to uproot myself like she did, jacking in a job not knowing, if I could get another one to, pay a mortgage.

9 Hospital Appointments

A few years later Valerie found a lump on her breast, and had it removed, along with glands under her left armpit. She had radio therapy in Inverness for a few weeks after that. That was tough going for her. Then I was called in for a health check, and found out I was diabetic, and was told to get my weight down, and change my diet. Changing my diet was OK, but getting my weight down was another thing. I was put on tablets for blood pressure. Then another nightmare for us, Valerie found another lump, this time on her neck. Back to the doctor, more tests. result thyroid cancer. Out to Dundee for an operation, and as there were no planes to Dundee, we decided to take the car and stop off to see the family in Glasgow. We stayed with our daughter for a night or two, and then drove to Dundee. Finding a place to stay was a bit of a problem, as we didn't know the area. I eventually found a place in a premier inn, while she was in for the operation. She went through the operation, but we found that it affected her voice which sometimes became hoarse. As we were travelling by car, they wouldn't let us travel up to Ullapool in one trip, so the decision was made for us to travel to Glasgow, and stay with our daughter for a week, then drive on. Coming off the motorway in Glasgow I was only a mile from our destination, I heard a clunking noise, and the engine stopped. I phoned my daughter to come and pick her mother up, and take her to her house, which she did. Lucky for me I had joined the A.A. the previous year, so I phoned them up, and he was there within a half hour. He took one look, and said, you can scrap it, the timing belt is broken, what next. I was paying out about a hundred pound a night on bed and breakfast in the premier inn for a week plus dinner and drinks on top of that, now I must pay out on a new car, things weren't working out very well. The A. A. towed me to my daughters, and the following day I went out and bought a wee Clio that I still have, that was an expensive trip. We arrived home about a week later.

At one of my appointments at the surgery, it was suggested that I could have Sleep Apnia, and I was referred to Raigmore. Another trip to hospital, which confirmed that I had. I was given a machine with a mask, which I must use when I go to sleep. While keeping tabs on my diabetes, I had an appointment to get my heart checked. Lying on the bed, with all these wires stuck to my body, I heard her say, oh, oh, we must get the heart nurse to see you. I had noticed I was getting breathless sometimes. The following morning a nurse came to the house, and gave me a tablet to swallow, and I was to take it immediately, she explained what was happening, and said I was to get a pacemaker fitted, what next. A trip out to Glasgow, which I didn't mind, as I could see the grand kids, then into the Jubilee a, lovely hospital, coming round after the operation, I was lying in bed, and my legs would not stay still, Crickey!! Is this what it's like to have a pacemaker? I called one of the nurses, and told her what was happening, and this chap came with what looked like a laptop. He laid a lead coming from it onto my pacemaker and proceeded to press some buttons, he explained what was happening, the pacemaker was fitted too close to some nerves, and every time I moved, it touched a nerve, and my legs would jump. A few twiddles on some knobs and that was it I was discharged the following day. Ten days later I walked Two miles to gallows hill and back. I was back to normal but must keep exercising.

On coming home from hospital, I found that Valerie had been admitted to hospital in Stornoway, after falling on the ice, and hurting her back. Valerie hadn't been feeling well, and she was back and fore to both Stornoway and Raigmore for various tests. At one time there was a competition as who had the most appointments. I woke up one morning about three Am, in severe pain, and went by ambulance to hospital about seven am, I was diagnosed with kidney stones. There was a Greek doctor on the ward, a nice fellow who has since sadly died. He told me to drink, keep drinking, in the end I said to him, I don't know who to believe, my wife keeps telling me to stop drinking. No, no, he said not that stuff, water. They flew me out to the Queen Elizabeth, in Glasgow by air ambulance, and that was when my troubles started. The operation went well, they fitted a stent in my urinal tubes to allow stones to pass and I was referred to Raigmore for them to be removed, three weeks later. While in the hospital, after my opp. I was sent to High Dependency Unit. I think they must have put another patient into my room. When they were going to discharge me, they didn't know how to, not only that, but they had lost all my clothes and belongings. They eventually found my belongings, but I was still stuck in HDU. I had blood tests every afternoon and the doctor would check it the following morning and gave me the OK to go. That happened three days on the run, but as they didn't know how to discharge me, I was stuck there. I asked to speak to a senior nurse, but she wouldn't come near me. Then a young female doctor came to speak to me and apologized. I explained that I was getting a blood test every afternoon and they would not let me go until the doctor saw the result the following day, and this was happening every day. She promised me she would come in at six in the morning and take the blood test in time for the other Doctor to get the result, which she did, and I was given the OK to go for the fourth time. I was getting frustrated by this time, and I asked for one of the nurses to speak to. I gave her all my particulars and a telephone number to ring, and ask for a travel warrant, I told her to go to her desk and to ring that number, which she did, fifteen minutes later she was back, and asked would the three o'clock plane the following day be, OK? I thanked her, and I was out the door and home. When I arrived home, I found Valerie had been admitted to hospital, after falling and hurting her shoulder, she seemed to land in hospital every time I went in. After all the tests she had she was diagnosed with Cancer in the bones and is now on a three-week course of tablets and injections once a month. She beat cancer twice before, and I know she can beat it a third time. I have been waiting for Raigmore to give me an appointment, for removing the stent, which was supposed to have been done a year ago. It finally arrived, I was to go out on Thursday and operation on Friday. Off on the plane in the morning and I went for my appointment at eight a.m. sitting in my gown and theatre socks waiting to go for my operation, guess what, a nurse came in and told me it was cancelled, no beds available. Well, I can't put in writing what my thoughts were, all that travelling and expense and everything else, It could only happen to me. I have just had another appointment, and must go for a covid test first, we shall see what the outcome will be. The test came back negative, so that is me on my way to Inverness for my opp. I had to go down the day before and stay in Kyle Court for the night as my appointment was at 7.30 am. I drove down to the airport on Thursday morning and left the car in the car park, thinking I could pick it up on Monday when I came off the flight. There were only four people on the plane, and I soon found myself in a taxi on the way to Raigmore. As I was staying in kyle court for the night, I had to find something to eat for my tea, although I had to starve myself later. I found a machine in the hospital that had sandwiches and took them with me to kyle court and had a cup of tea, most of them landed in the bin. After a shower and a glass of water in the morning I walked over to the hospital giving myself plenty of time to find where I was supposed to go. I found ward 3c very quickly and just sat outside until just before my appointment. After a while I was called in and taken to a one bed ward, where they started asking all kinds of questions that they normally do when going for any operation. Then into my gown ready for theatre, within two hours of arriving, I was on my way for surgery. As I woke up, I realized I was in a different ward, this was an open ward with three other patients. I was still in agony and in ward 4c which I think was a recovery ward and given pain killers, which didn't seem to work at first. So, they gave me more which made everything go fuzzy, and I was out of it. When I woke up, I was OK for a while, and then the pain started again and more pain killers. As I lay groaning in bed I could hear this fellow in the bed beside me, I couldn't help hearing him as he had a voice that carried, and you could hear everything he said. He was in conversation with the patient opposite him about fishing, and where he stayed, he never stopped talking except when the nurses came in. He was from North Uist and called McVicar. One nurse came in and asked how long had he been in the water? I didn't get his answer as I was bent double with pain, he was diabetic and must have had a hypo and blacked out, the next thing I heard the nurse saying, "what have you got there in that lemonade bottle"? and then she shouted at him, "That's whisky, no wonder we can't regulate your bloods, how did you get that in here". The chap opposite him was called Ali, and he burst out laughing and shouted you have been caught out McVicar, that kept him quiet for a while, but then it came round to fishing again. He must have had an omelette for his tea for in the middle of his conversation with Ali he said, "I wish I could make an omelette", Ali said "that's easy enough, all you need is heat up your pan two eggs and two spoonsful of milk". "Is that all", he said, "I must try it when I get home". Then the conversation came back to fishing. A couple of hours later he said to Ali, "what do you do with the two spoonsful of water"? "What spoonful of water"? "That you have with the eggs", Its two spoonsful of milk, not water". "Oh yes, two spoonsful of milk", and then the conversation came back to fishing and the lochs they fished. Sometime the following day, I had just been given more pain killers and was lying in bed groaning, waiting for them to take effect, when out of the blue he said to Ali, "what do you do with the milk"? "You mix it with the eggs and heat it up". "Oh, you mix the two together, oh I see, yes yes". I would like to see that omelette when he is finished, but it kept my mind off my pain for a while. Sometime later, or the following day I am not sure, the consultant came around along with three or four doctors and nurses, to tell me how things had gone. As he started to tell me, I told him I couldn't hear him, as McVicar was on the phone, and everybody on the ward could hear what he was saying. One of the nurses put her head round and told him to be quiet as they were in consultation. Well, the following conversation could have been taken out of a carry-on film. He shouted, "sorry, doctor, Sorry". "Annie, I have to go, sorry, sorry doctor", as he put his head round the curtain "Annie oh it's Mary, Sorry doctor sorry", as he put his head round the curtain again, "Mary, could you tell Murdo Sorry, doctor sorry", "Could you tell Murdo to put the sheep", and at this point one of the other doctors put her head round the screen and shouted "McVicar, be quiet". "Oh, sorry doctor sorry, Mary, I have to go there's a right tartar here today". I was looking at the consultant and I think he was about to pee himself trying not to laugh. I heard him say to one of the young doctors he was going for something he had left behind, the other doctor offered to go for it, but he said no for them to stay, and he would not be long. The consultant told me that when they had the result of the x-ray, they saw I had a massive stone in my bladder and rather than try and get the stent out they concentrated on blasting this stone, which was about four inches in diameter. As it took them three hours to get rid of that stone, they couldn't risk having me under for longer, as it was too dangerous. So the stent is still in with a stone attached, to be taken out at a later date. I was still in pain as my tubes were still blocked and I was kept on pain killers and hadn't eaten in about four days. Eventually on Tuesday as I was still in pain, they did what you call a Nephrostomy, which is a pipe going into my back into my kidney to allow me to pee, I was wide awake when that was done. Lying on my stomach on a stretcher I could feel them working on my back, took about twenty minutes, then back to the ward. Within an hour I could feel the pain subsiding, which was a relief. I was told this is only temporary, and I would have to go back for the stent removal in about a fortnight or three weeks' time. Two days later I was on the plane home with an extra bag beside me. I had originally booked to come back on Monday that had to be cancelled and then it was Wednesday and finally Thursday. I have the nurse coming in once a week, to change my dressing, until I get my next appointment. After I came back, I was sorry to hear that my old playmate Hector, had passed away. Two days after the nurse had changed my dressing, I felt my shirt wet, and realized that the Nephrostomy was not working, and was leaking on my back. I called the nurse and as she looked at it, she had to phone the doctor, as she couldn't do anything with it. Into hospital again and with some discussion with Raigmore decided to fly me out there for treatment. Off by air ambulance Saturday morning, I arrived at Inverness airport and had to wait for about three quarters of an hour for an ambulance to pick me up, if I had gone on the ordinary flight and a taxi, I could have been in hospital an hour ago. Arriving in Raigmore I had to have a covid test before being admitted and the result came back an hour later as negative. I was put in ward 6c and told it would be at least Tuesday before I would be operated on. Monday I was transferred to ward 4c as they were quite busy and needed my bed. That was the ward I was in before and I met the same nurses again. I was still getting pains and was told to keep drinking. Wednesday I was put on fluids only, which was a good sign, and then nil by mouth which was a good sign that something was happening. Two pm and I was on my way to theatre and came back to the ward at eight pm with no pain and no bag beside me. The following morning, I had breakfast and was told I was being discharged that day, as everything had worked out OK. Taxi to the airport and the plane home. Two days later I had a phone call from the Cardio Department at Raigmore, asking if I was OK, "yes", I said, "why"? "We have no response from the Heart Monitor". I explained that I had been out in Raigmore. As I didn't have the Machine with me at the hospital, it was too far away to pick up any signal, at least somebody is looking after me. I was wondering afterwards what if I had said no, what would be their reaction. Two months later I had a call from the local hospital, would I call in the following morning at eight thirty for an appointment at the Cardio Department. They put some leads on to the Pacemaker and twiddled a few knobs on what looked like a laptop. They said my own heart was trying to take over, and they didn't want that. They wanted the pacemaker to do the work. Technology or what.

10 Redundancy to Self-Employment

Kenny, my boss was past retiring age, and one day he called us in and told us he was retiring and would have to make us redundant. Well after working for the same firm for over 30 years I didn't know what to do. The day after I received my redundancy, I called into the job centre. I had an interview there first, asked all kinds of stupid questions, and had to practically tell them my whole life story, as the last time I was in there was when I left school. In the three or four days I kept going in, they never once offered me a job. I made the decision then to start up on my own. I had some cards printed with my name and phone number, and distributed them round the town, within a day I had my first call, and I was only off one day without a job, until I retired. One job I had; it was a house out in the country which I had to renovate for a lady on the mainland. I fitted new windows, a new kitchen new bathroom and a stair up to another bedroom. Sending her photos of each stage by e-mail and getting paid regularly. I never met her until it was finished. The best job I had was for a German lady, she was the boss of a large factory in Germany making office furniture. They had offices in London, and a few other European countries. She had brought up her two granddaughters after their parents were killed in a car crash, and this was the youngest, who was married with three children all under school age. I was given instructions from the granddaughter but had to be confirmed by a phone call or e-mail from Germany. She was very good at paying, as soon as I sent her an e-mail and an invoice, the money was in my account within two days. I supplied and fitted a new kitchen and bathroom, supplied, and fitted new curtains throughout, and even arranged for a new drive from the road into the house with a turning point. An amusing incident occurred one day, while I was showing her a catalogue of doors that she wanted to renew. The lady was quite tall, six feet something, and as I sat on the couch she sat beside me, while breast feeding the youngest, I turned round to show her some doors that would be suitable, and at that precise moment ,she was changing the child from her left to her right breast, and her left breast nearly went in to my eye, she just giggled, and said sorry, as I rubbed my right eye to try and focus. I looked at her husband, who was standing in front of me, and he didn't bat an eye as he was looking at the other catalogue. I met the lady just once, when she came up for a few days with her other granddaughter and husband, they lived in London.

Now, Valerie is on ten or twelve tablets a day, as well as her chemo tablets plus her monthly injections, so her immune system is very low. Recently we noticed her going to the toilet quite frequently, and through the night. As I got out of bed one morning she was coming back from the toilet and did not have the strength to climb back into bed. I helped her in and went to phone the doctor, as this was a weekend there were no doctors available, so I dialled 111 Fifteen minutes on the phone and nobody answering, eventually somebody came on the line, and I explained what was wrong, after about ten minutes of questions and answers she said, I shall go and get a nurse to speak to you. Who in heavens name was I talking to? A nurse then came on the line and started asking me the same questions, after nearly an hour I put down the phone, and dialed 999 They were in the house within ten minutes, and off to hospital, diagnosed with a severe urine infection, and was kept in for a couple of days. A couple of months later I had to get in touch with a doctor urgently, and again was told to dial 111 This time when I dialed, I was told it would be 90 minutes before my call would be answered, you can guess what my thoughts were, what an emergency number. With today`s technology you would think they could get a better system than that. Even Alexa can tell me what kind of day it's going to be. I know the older generation used to talk about the good old days, I know what they meant, as my younger years were the best.

11 Tales from my Elders

In one of the houses, we used to go to celebrate New Year was Murdo, we shall call him Murdo for the purpose of the story. He was about twenty-five years older than I, but we had a good time with plenty of crack and music. He came from a large family, and on one Sunday their mother had a salmon in the pot for dinner, and told them to look after it, while she and their dad went to church. Salmon does not take long to cook and the smell of it made them hungry, so they started nibbling at it, until they realized there was nothing left for their mum and dad, and they would all be in trouble, nothing for it, they had to get another one and fast ,as they lived near the river two of them ran off, and took another one from the river, ran back home, gutted it and put in the pot just in time to be cooked before their mum and dad came home. As their mother started sharing out the salmon, she looked a bit bemused and said, I have cooked a few salmon that came from that river, but this is the first I have seen with two heads, they had forgotten to take the other head out.

They used to go to keose road end on a Friday night to the dancing, and Murdo`s sisters kept telling him to go home as he was too young, so he decided to get his own back on them. He waited till it was dark and took the sheep dog, and a bed sheet, and went down near to where they were dancing. He tied the bed sheet round the dog's neck and let him loose, with all the hilarity the dog thought this was a game and ran off in among them, as the dog was black all they could see was the white sheet, and they took off screaming, as the dog knew them, he followed them thinking this was a great game. I don't know what the outcome was as they ran into the house screaming and the dog followed them. If you did something like that today, you would be charged with assault.

One of the travelling people was taken to court for some misdemeanoror other and he was taken in front of the sheriff, and the conversation went like this. The sheriff asked him, "What is your name"? "Donald Macdonald my lord". "Are you married"? "Yes, my lord". "Who too"? "A woman my lord". "Is that right, have you ever heard of anyone being married to a man"? "Yes, my lord". "Who"? "My sister, my lord". That was the end of that conversation.

There is a story told to me by my elders about an old man, who lived on a small island called the Noonan, you can still see the remains of his house , he had a salmon net stretched from the Noonan across to another island, when he went to bed he would tie the rope of the net to his big toe, so when a salmon went into the net the struggling and pulling on the net would wake him up. You can believe that or not. I always wondered as that island goes under at high tide it must have been vastly different a few hundred years ago, as there is still grass growing there.

Two men from the village, keen poachers. Murdo and Tom used to go out together, for some reason, only known to him, Tom decided to take up the job of a watcher for the gamekeeper. One of the lookout spots was a hill just beside the cemetery, as he could look down on the river and see anybody that came along. Murdo knew this, whether he was going poaching on his own we don't know, as he made his way through the cemetery, he saw Tom on the skyline, and made his way up to him, and lay down beside him. Tom was probably half asleep and didn't notice him. At about one or two in the morning. Murdo realizing Tom hadn't seen him, tapped him on the shoulder and said, do you see anything Tom? The next thing Tom was on his feet, and ready to take to the hills, thinking somebody had come up from the grave. I am sure there were a few curses and swears directed at his mate.

There was a tale about a poacher from the village out on the river one day with a gaff, hoping to catch a salmon. when he saw the lady who owned the estate, lady something or other, and two gamekeepers coming into sight, as he had no time to dispose of the gaff without them seeing him, he opened his trousers and bent down and held the gaff under water as if he was opening his bowels, when the lady eventually saw him all she saw was a bare backside, and she made an about turn and walked back the way she came.

In an incident over in Ness at one of the bochans, which was an illegal drinking den, which was quite often raided by the police. A group of teenagers went to the bochan one night, and as one of them was only sixteen they wouldn't let him in, but he was given a half pint, and told to stay outside, and keep a look out for any cars coming. He was quite happy with that and kept watch. Eventually a car turned into the road, and he shouted a warning to those inside. What is the number plate on it? Someone asked I don't know, I can't make it out, Oh yes, its p, o, l, one, c, e. Panic stations.!!!

12 My Mad Days

When Hector got married, they held the reception in the town hall. Sometimes other people would come to the dance and create havoc, so it was decided to make it ticket only. Halfway through the night I was asked if I could relieve the fellow at the side door, with strict instructions not to let anybody in without a ticket. I was only on for about ten minutes, when two ladies came along and tried to get in. When I asked them for their ticket, one of them tried to push me to one side, and I stepped in front to stop her, eventually someone told me it was the bride's mother and her friend. I get reminded about that every so often. I just say I was given strict instructions not let anybody in without a ticket.

We had great fun in our teenage years riding our bikes up and down the road, and through the village, we didn't see having lights or torches on our bikes as a necessity, until one night a big van forced us off the road, and into the ditch. We looked up and saw police written on the side, that was it we looked at each other and took off, each going in different directions. We all had the same thought; we didn't want to have our names in the police black book. As I shot off, out the road to the peats I saw that the policeman was chasing me and was about twenty yards behind me. No way was he going to get a hold of me, so I ditched the bike, and ran into the moor, knowing that he would not follow me and get his feet wet. From then on, most of us had either a torch or dynamo, on our bikes, my one and only encounter with the law, I think. I was riding home on a dark night, I could only see where I was going by watching the fence posts, on either side of the road, and could make out their outline, until all of a sudden an outline appeared in front of me, and I pulled on my brakes and found myself stopping with my front wheel in between my father's legs, I got a clout behind my ears and was told to get off home. Another time on a similar night, I arrived home and was making myself a cup of tea, when my mother walked in, she asked me, had I just come in the road? I said "yes, why"? Something hit my shoulder as I came in the road, and I never heard anything. I never let on, but something hit me as well, after that episode I went and bought myself a torch for my bike. Another episode comes to mind, riding our bikes we decided to cycle down to Soval lodge, as we knew that four girls had started there as house maids for the summer. Sneaking round the lodge we found out where their bedrooms were, and there was an open window. Very tempting to us, as myself and one of my mates climbed in and jumped into bed with two of them. We didn't last very long there, as with all the giggling and squealing from the girls, it alerted the head house maid. As we heard her coming down the hall shouting about the carry on, we made a quick exit out the window as she came in the door. When she saw us, she did an about turn to block us off, which she did as we were in a sort of back yard with only one exit. We knew who she was as she was from laxay, but we didn't want her to know who we were. It was getting quite dark, so we were able to dodge her, though every time she saw us, she flapped a towel at us, whatever the towel was going to do I don't know. We eventually escaped and caught up with the other two and cycled off home, thinking, if only.

A similar escapade happened when we were coming home from a jaunt to town. I Can't remember who was with me, but we decided for devilment to go into a house on Cameron terrace. We knew the family, because we used to call there most Fridays and pick their girls up and take them to the dances. This night the house was in darkness as they had probably gone to bed, but the front door wasn't locked, so we crept in and sneaked upstairs. We had no sooner got into the bedroom when we heard her mother shouting, "who is there"? It was time to get out of there, as we ran downstairs with their mother chasing us, and out the door, shouting she was getting the police. As we knew them very well, I decided to go back and apologize, I got a clip over the head, and asked in for a cup of tea.

My father died in1986 of heart failure, and my mother two years later in 1988. after a stroke. I lost my two brothers a few years back, the eldest in 2005 to Cancer and my other brother in 2011 also from cancer sad days in my life.

There are two things that annoy me in life, when I phone somebody, and I am answered by a machine, which tells me to press one for this, press two for that and three for something else. and plastic gadgets that don't last.

I was born as the Second World War ended and I count myself extremely lucky, I have lived through constantly improving times. Life is much easier than in my parent's day. I was brought up to respect others, regardless of race or social status. My parent's generation learned the hard way that war is never the solution to our problems. Equality and mutual respect are far more effective than violence and hate.

Closing Thoughts

This page should have been page twenty, but things keep coming back to me. You may find some of these episodes or stories or whatever you want to call them, unbelievable, but all are true, and nothing is added or exaggerated, apart from a few jokes I added in. I see the difference in generations, when I was growing up, if I was looking for my mates I would knock on their door, walk in, and shout their name. If I didn't get an answer, I walked out the back door to see if they were in the back garden. If no one was home, you closed the door behind you, and tried the next house. Nowadays, every door is locked. Hopefully by reading this book, the next generation can see how we were brought up, and made our own amusement, rather than sitting in front of a television or with computer games.

When I retired at sixty-five, I started thinking of what I was going to do for the rest of my life, sitting in front of a T.V. was not an option. I decided to take up a hobby, and genealogy came to mind, and as I got into it and learned more about my ancestors, I kept thinking back to my own life, and had a wee laugh at some of my memories. This gave me the idea of sharing my memories with others. When you reach a certain age, you wish you could remember more, ask your parents and grandparents about their lives. If only they had written things down, they might not be lost, forever. Although I am not a fan of computers, it helped me put my memories down in writing. I hope that this will be a legacy for my children and remind us of all the people who made us into who we are today.

Family Tree

Great-grandparents:

Torquil Macleod (1811-1890) - Ann Macleod (1811-1883)

Donald Macleod (1800-?) - Margaret Macleod (1800-?)

Malcolm Macleod (1837-1913) - Catherine Maciver (1840-1928)

Duncan Macleod (1840-1934) - Chirsty Macritchie (1841-1916)

Grandparents:

Malcolm Macleod (1869-1953) - Euphemia Macinnes (1871-1926)
John Macleod (1871-1916) - Hannah Macleod (1877-1962)

Parents:

Torquil Macleod (1903-1986) - Margaret Macleod (1905-1988)

Me:

Malcolm Macleod (1946-)

Printed in Great Britain
by Amazon